THEKITCHEN

CREATING CONTEMPORARY HOMES

THE KITCHEN

VINNY LEE Photography by Andrew Wood

jacqui
small

First published in 2003 by
Jacqui Small
an imprint of Aurum Press Limited
7 Greenland Street
London NW1 0ND

This paperback edition published in 2007

Publisher: Jacqui Small
Design: Ghost Design
Editor: Sian Parkhouse
Location researcher: Nadine Bazaar
Production: Geoff Barlow

ISBN-10:1 903221 54 4
SIBN-13: 978 1 903221 54 9

A catalogue record for this book is
available from the British Library

Printed in China

2009 2008 2007
10 9 8 7 6 5 4 3 2 1

To AWJ – a vital ingredient

contents

INTRODUCTION

Successful kitchen design is all about problem solving as well as customizing a space to suit your lifestyle. To do this well, you must identify your needs, assess your budget and the space within which you have to work, and choose the correct hardware that will enable the kitchen to function efficiently. Style and decoration are important, but they are the final phases, the finishing touches that are applied once the basic architectural and mechanical elements are in place.

In this book, we start by focusing on the practical aspects of kitchen design and show how individuals have, in their own homes, addressed and tackled most common kitchen-planning dilemmas. With the help of some leading architects and designers and their innovative solutions, we show how small rooms were enlarged, large ones sub-divided into more manageable kitchens, dark places given light, and awkward spaces made to conform. In the second part of the book, we look closely at the individual components which contribute to the functioning of the kitchen, and in the last section we address fine tuning and personalizing.

Putting together a scheme for a kitchen is similar to tackling a giant jigsaw. Many facets, like the blue sky in a puzzle, appear the same, but are in fact subtly different, so it takes patience to select the right piece and sometimes an amount of manoeuvring to get it into the correct place. Also, like the puzzle, it is important to get the framework right: all the perimeters should be lined up and perfect before the full picture can be seen, and any pieces incorrectly aligned will inevitably cause repercussions across the board.

But planning and fitting a kitchen is no game, it is a significant undertaking and a considerable investment in your home as well as one that requires careful planning and organization. Although the kitchen is the most practical room in a home, where the basic act of providing food is undertaken, it has also become one of the most technological sites. Recent advances in appliances and finishes have made it an increasingly sophisticated place, although another aspect of good kitchen design is to make it seem less so.

Once planning problems and machine selection have been tackled and solved, the aim should be to create a room that not only functions efficiently and is a pleasure to work in, but is also a place where you, your family and friends enjoy spending time.

Left: Increasingly in modern homes, the functions of the kitchen and dining rooms are combined. Here an open-plan living area accommodates the two purposes in one space, creating a contemporary multi-purpose room where socializing and food preparation can take place at the same time.

The Casebook

This page: As the kitchen has become a more public space, its décor has grown in importance. The choice of fascias and finishes has multiplied, and furniture is designed to be less utilitarian and more aesthetic.

Right: Small display areas where china and glassware can be shown as an integral part of the overall scheme are increasingly popular. The position and lighting of these cabinets will make them a focal point.

Below right: Surfaces such as this glass worktop that doubles as an informal dining area must withstand the daily routine of food preparation and cleaning, but also look presentable as an area on which to dine.

sink and dishwasher. The standard formating and layout for these functions revolves around what is known as 'the work triangle'.

The work triangle places each one of the functions at a separate point, and the distance between each should be manageable, so that you are not walking and carrying things over long distances or around hazards such as steps. The functions are connected – you wash and prepare food and then take it to the oven or hob, and also take dirty pans from the hob to the sink – so the layout should allow for the pathway between each point to be accessible and clear.

In many modern kitchens the work triangle becomes contorted, especially in the galley or linear kitchen, where functions may run along one surface, side by side, or in a large kitchen where it may be necessary to introduce an island unit to enclose and contain the facilities. Sometimes the cooking functions may be divided, with a wall-mounted oven on one side and the hob against the opposite wall. The shape may also need to bend and adapt to avoid having a main entrance and traffic route going through the centre.

THE BASICS

In this first section of the book, we look at real case studies where architects and designers have worked together with their clients to solve problems and make the best kitchen or kitchen-dining area possible in the space available. From the examples of the kitchens people have made in their homes, we will see how function and form can be brought together to create practical, attractive rooms.

As the role of the kitchen has expanded to include dining, living and family activities, its looks and layout have also had to change dramatically. Few kitchens are now used solely for food preparation – most have a least a small table for casual dining. The barriers between rooms are now frequently demolished, to create open-plan living. Problems associated with the kitchen – smells, dampness and the accumulation of grease – still dog us, but with improved ventilation and easy wipe-clean surfaces, these tribulations are being reduced. As the kitchen has also acquired the role of dining space, the overall decoration and styling of the room has had to accommodate not only practical features for cooking, but also the more decorative elements required for entertaining. It has become a many-faceted room in more ways than one.

Whether your kitchen is small, large or multi-functional, the basic elements are the same. You will need an area for food preparation, which will include or be close to food storage and a fridge; next there is the hot area – oven, hob and a grill; then the water section with

Left: A feature of the modern extended kitchen is the need for additional space to accommodate a dining function. Here a narrow table and a pair of bench seats mirror the size and location of the island unit.

Below: Although they are in a modern-style kitchen, these open shelves serve the same purpose, and have a similar appearance to, the traditional kitchen dresser.

Bottom: An existing fireplace has been kept as a feature in this kitchen, adding a softer, more domesticated feel to the room.

Right: Instead of using high stools with a tall breakfast bar to create additional dining space, in this kitchen the surface is at a lower level and can be used with more traditional style seats.

Kitchen design is constantly being updated as fashions change and technology advances. Among the latest trend is to dispense with plinths and kickboards, and support base units on legs or cantilever them from the wall so that they appear to float above the floor. In a similar vein, the floating shelf has come into its own; although it is attached by brackets slotted into the back of the shelf, there is no visible means of support. The advancements in glass technology have also brought this material, reinforced and laminated, into the kitchen, adding an airiness that can be an asset in small or ill-lit spaces.

After years of soft pastel colours and minimalist white and steel, vibrant colour has also marched back into the kitchen. Brightly coloured panels, whether painted or in sections of bright laminates, are giving the kitchen a new, more exciting appearance.

But a well-planned kitchen should not be a fashion-victim. It is good to introduce the most up-to-date elements of design and technology, but the kitchen is an expensive and time-consuming room to construct. It should have a classic appearance that can be altered and updated by means of well-chosen accessories, rather than costly units and flooring that will be distruptive to change.

SELECTING A STYLE

Although the architectural input to a kitchen is important, it is the decoration that really adds or defines the style. It is not just the colour or finish you choose; it is the smaller things that all go to create a definitive look.

There are numerous styles or looks to choose from when decorating a kitchen and the problem is often deciding which one to select. Some people follow a scheme sympathetic to the architectural period of their home or of a time that they admire or feel an affinity to, for example Art Deco or Arts and Crafts. Other people choose a style that reminds them of a place they like – that is why you can come across a Mediterranean style kitchen in the centre of London, Swedish or Gustavian-inspired rooms in Manhattan and Shaker kitchens in Paris.

required to be able to live like this but there are variations on the theme that are less demanding. The interest in the professional-style kitchen, using industrial materials such as concrete, cookers with six burner rings and steel-fronted units, is also a hard look, but it can be adapted and softened to work in a more family-orientated home.

There is also the option to mix and match different styles and create your own individual look but there are rules and guidelines to be followed otherwise there is a danger of creating a mess. Start with a neutral base,

The rustic or traditional look has long been popular with those who like the idea of baking their own bread and making preserves and pickles, the way their grandmother did, but for most people living and working in today's high-speed world the decorative scheme of their kitchen is about as close as they will get to the rustic dream.

The contemporary kitchen pared down to its purist form is a clean, angular workstation. Most gadgets and implements are stored out of sight and surfaces are kept spotlessly clean. A disciplined mind is

a blank canvas, and then add your decorative elements. Try to keep embellishments within a restricted palette of two or three colours. Often you only need a few key pieces to establish a style; for example, in a rustic kitchen a dresser is an essential, and Shaker style is most often represented by a peg rail and the use of specific colours – ox-blood red, sage green and blue. The advantage of this approach is that when you grow tired of the look you don't need to re-decorate from top to bottom – simply update it by changing the accessories.

CONTEMPORARY sleek

Due to planning restrictions the exterior of this newly built house had to be designed in a traditional style, but the interior is unflinchingly contemporary. Working with architect John Pawson, the owner created a kitchen wiith a minimal appearance, but a wall of floor-to-ceiling cupboards contain every element of storage and machinery found in a regular fully operational kitchen.

PLAN

1 Featureless floor-to-ceiling cupboards
2 Recessed oblong sinks
3 Multi-purpose island unit
4 Four-panel recessed ceramic hob and hot plate
5 Separate formal dining area

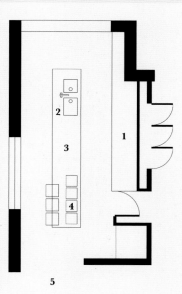

Minimalism

A flat wall of panelled doors (left) conceals all storage, the dishwasher, refrigerator as well as an additional worktop. The central island work station holds a double sink and a ceramic hob.

Sliding doors

The panel doors slide back into recesses (above) so they do not impinge on the floor space when they are open.

Materials

The kitchen is linked to a dining area (right). Because the rooms are quite small the architect and the owner decided to keep the number of different finishes to a minimum. The worktop in the kitchen and the hearth in the living area are made from the same Italian grey stone, Petraserene.

THE CASEBOOK

The owner of this kitchen, which was put into a newly built house five years ago, is a keen cook, and when in use the surfaces in the kitchen are utilized extensively, but after the preparation work is done and the meal is finished everything is returned to its place and the recessed panel cupboard doors are pulled out and closed over the wall of shelves, machines and storage, creating an immaculate, starkly furnished room.

The secret to this kitchen is the concealed storage; there is plenty of it, but when the doors are closed it is invisible. On the outer surface the panel doors are faced with matt lacquer, but the inner surfaces are covered with practical Formica. When opened, the doors slide back into recesses so that the whole of the inner surface can be exposed and the contents viewed. The doors and shelves are 3cm (1½in) thick, a third wider than the average specification – this was selected by the architect, and the owner says that it helps to give a more luxurious feel and appearance to the storage system.

In contrast to the sophisticated design and finish of the kitchen, the floor is in plain, unfinished oak laid in long straight boards, which, according to the owner, has aged well, and it is easily maintained by simply washing down with soap and water.

Beautiful and practical
One of the two large rectangular sinks (left) has a waste disposal system that can be used even while the sink is full of dishes or water.

Concealed machines
All the white goods in this kitchen, such as the dishwasher and the coffee-maker, for example (above), are contained within the cupboard space. The dishwasher has been raised from floor level so that you do not have to bend or stoop to load and unload it, and the coffee-maker is at eye level, which makes it simple and safe to use.

CLEAN LINES

The thick Italian stone work surface on the central island unit has an overhang at one corner, to allow space for four stools to sit snugly underneath – this provides an area for casual dining in the kitchen or for friends to sit and chat while a meal is being prepared. All the shapes and materials are strictly clean and unfussy. The stools are very simple oak cubes, open on one side so they are light enough to be lifted, and they echo the chunky feel of the worktop. The operating controls for the ceramic hobs, like the lever taps for the sinks at the other end of the unit, are situated below the rim of the worktop, so the surface is free of knobs and handles.

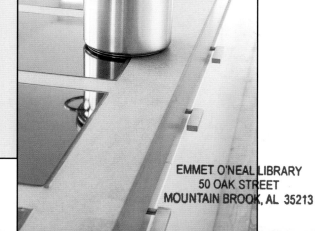

MODERN rustic

Although this house was built in the 1960s, the kitchen looks as though it is much older, and yet it conceals all the facilities and conveniences of a modern kitchen. This convincing rustic appearance has been achieved through close attention to detail and clever surface treatments. The kitchen opens onto an informal dining space decorated in a more sophisticated but sympathetic style; painted terracotta floor tiles help to link both areas.

PLAN

1 Floor-standing cooker with integral hob
2 Refrigerator, freezer and storage unit with distressed fascia panel
3 An adapted table used as a narrow central work area
4 Old-style ceramic Belfast sink
5 Circular dining table
6 Traditional-style dresser

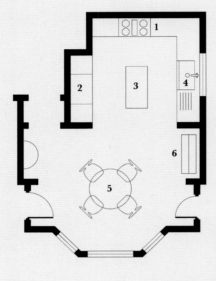

Linking areas

The view through to the dining area shows the base of the substantial beam that helps to delineate the different functions of the two areas, while the use of sympathetic furnishings and finishes links the two spaces. Light linen chair covers and floor-length drapes lend an appearance of sophistication to the dining area, whereas the aged cupboard doors in the kitchen endorse the rustic theme.

Detailing

Every part of the decoration has been carefully thought through, even down to the neat regularly spaced nail heads and the choice of small round drawer handles (above right). It is the sum of these individual components that gives a complete and finished appearance (opposite).

In creating this adjoining kitchen and dining space various decorating techniques have been used to define and separate the two areas, yet to provide a visual and thematic link. This is important because the rooms are clearly visible one from the other, but they are not big spaces, so to decorate each in completely different or contrasting schemes would create a barrier and also make each room appear smaller.

One of the techniques used to separate the spaces is an angular arch incorporating an old beam; this creates a strong visual divide. But the same terracotta floor tiles run

MATERIALS

The cabinets were made locally and the standard panelled doors were then aged by hand, bleached and painted with soft washes of colour. The splashback is covered with tumbled limestone mosaic, with a naturally aged appearance and subtle colouring. These tiles have also been used on the upper surface of the open shelves, which are made from old scaffolding boards cantilevered from the wall. The thick shelves run on either side of the cooker, and echo the size and proportions of the beam in the archway. The cooker hood has been finished with a broad beam trim to continue the visual line of the adjacent shelves.

between the two spaces. Originally new and bright red-orange; the tiles have been painted with a soft grey wash to bring down the redness and then sealed with a mat wax-like finish. The unusual honeycomb shape adds to the decorative appearance of the room. In the dining room, a round rug softens and refines that area as well as echoing the shape of the table.

The walls in the kitchen are covered with a textured cement scratch coat but in the dining area there is a smoother, more polished finish. Important in both rooms are displays of china, but in the kitchen the tableware perches on thick beam shelves whereas in the dining area the display is in an original Charlottesville cupboard.

Another link between the rooms is the central island. This was installed to extend the work surface and to aid the function of a working triangle. Instead of conventional cupboards or a butcher's block an antique

tilt-top wine-tasting table was selected. The narrow structure allows for movement either side, and its open base makes it appear more as an attractive piece of furniture than a unit when viewed from the dining table.

The kitchen itself is not large but it has been well planned with plenty of concealed storage (important to keep mundane things from sight of the dining room), as well as open shelves for displaying more graceful and interesting old and new china and tableware. Modern machines such as the refrigerator and freezer are concealed behind wooden panel doors treated and painted to match the rest of the units.

Freestanding furniture

The Charlottesville dresser (left) is original, but a subtle toile paper has been used to line the back and introduce an element of pattern into what is otherwise a simple and plainly coloured scheme.

WORKTOPS

The muted and patinated traditional zinc work surface was wrapped over pre-cut prepared plywood bases and then secured in place using old-fashioned roofing tacks. The tacks remain visible and are a key part of the decorative scheme. Zinc has a bluish-white mottled appearance, and was often used as a roofing material and in printing plates; it is a durable and hard-wearing surface so it ages well and has a reasonably soft handle that allows it to be rolled and hammered into place. The sink is also in keeping with the traditional style; a deep ceramic Belfast design with a swan-neck spout and ceramic taps.

Dining

The owner of this kitchen loves to eat and entertain, but is not too fond of the process of cooking, so the food preparation area is small and the dining table dominates the floor space (above). The large cooker is used to heat up prepared dishes and there is ample storage for china, cutlery and glassware.

Flooring

Reed and coir mats with bound edges (above right) define dining and seating areas. This adds softness and prevents the space from being too noisy and cold.

FUSION style

The Oriental theme, colouring and style is carried through from the kitchen to the other rooms in this loft apartment. Maple flooring and cabinets give a warm tone to the scheme, which complements rather than contrasts with black granite worktops. Matt-finish steel splashbacks add a contemporary and durable aspect and the angular modern dining table reflects the linear shape of the kitchen plan and the archway opening to adjacent rooms.

The black surfaces echo the thick wooden shelves, made from old railway sleepers, in the adjoining seating area, and harmonize with the eastern and contemporary furniture. They also pick up on dark wooden beams exposed during the renovation of this 19th-century industrial sugar refinery. Solid custom-made wooden base and wall cabinets have simple steel handles that leave the surfaces uncluttered. Chinese 18th-century chairs are arranged around a table designed by the owner in solid oak stained dark grey and set on a steel base.

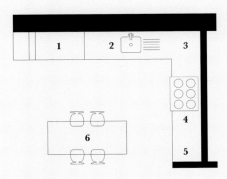

PLAN

1 Refrigerator recessed into units

2 Sink with single lever tap in front of stainless steel splashback

3 Black granite worktop area

4 Oven and hob

5 Unit containing deep shelf storage

6 Contemporary dining table with classic Oriental chairs

Machines

A good-size refrigerator for storing prepared foods and salads was important in a space that is used primarily for entertaining. But this kitchen is quite small so a very large refrigerator could have been overwhelming. To help make it part of the overall scheme, and appear to reduce its prominance and size in the room, it has been built into the run of wall-mounted and floor-standing cabinets (below). The solid steel door conceals the contents and marries up with the steel of the splashback, which also helps to reduce its presence.

Utensils on display
A collection of copper pans (originally from Russia but purchased in Finland) are not just decorative; they are used on an almost daily basis, so they maintain their well polished and shining finish (below and right).

Custom-built storage
The owner had this dresser custom made to fit the wall space (opposite), to house her collection of plates and china. Each meal involves at least six place settings for her large family, so she needs a lot of tableware.

Modern country

The owner of this kitchen is a keen cook who has four children. When structural renovation to the rest of her house meant she was able to move her kitchen she took the opportunity to create a large practical space to suit her lifestyle. But she also had an extensive collection of old and new china and glassware; creating custom-built storage to display this collection became the starting point for a decorative scheme that is simple and light, making it an enjoyable space to work and relax in.

PLAN
1 Site-specific custom-made dresser
2 Freestanding cooker and hob
3 Single sink used in conjunction with a large dishwasher
4 Tall island unit used for food preparation and casual dining
5 More formal dining area

While she was planning structural work, the owner decided a much larger kitchen was necessary for her to prepare meals for her, her husband and their four children. Rather than compromise on the existing space in the house she opted to knock through and convert an attached outbuilding.

The original smaller kitchen was due to be demolished when the space it occupied became a hallway. The new location for the kitchen was an adjacent one-time garage and workshop. The structure was in a 'raw' state; it had to be fully insulated and have windows fitted. Then the ceiling was removed to open the roof space and beams were installed – they were architecturally necessary but they also enhance the country-style appearance of the room and increase the feeling of light and space. Once this structural work was completed the resulting open space was divided into a dining area and a kitchen.

The decorative theme was kept simple and white to unify the whole room. This unfussy scheme also keeps the appearance light and fresh, which provides an excellent background for the more decorative items, such as the wide array of copper pans, the displays of tableware and antique Finnish cabinets. These wonderful old wooden cupboards have had most of the surface colours stripped away, but faint traces of the original paint colour survive in the grain.

Functional elegance
If your tableware is to be on permanent display it should be attractive as well as practical. The pure white colour of these china bowls (below) highlights the decorative scalloped shape.

Pretty touches
Small cameo displays of everyday items are very appealing. Mixing old and new objects can be done successfully as long as there is some compatibility, theme or connection between them. Here, an old silver tea strainer and some condiment containers are arranged on a white marble slab (right) and are mirrored in the reflection of a silver-plated tray.

COLOUR

The success of this contemporary take on a country style lies in the neutral background. The clean and simple decorative scheme provides a flattering background for the owner's collection of old and new china, antique and contemporary chairs and modern and classic lighting. The predominant colour is white and the abundance of high-gloss finishes reflect plenty of light. The white lacquer surface of the table, for example, is hardwearing and easy to clean but acts like a crisp white table cloth when set with china, glass and cutlery. Three old wooden Finnish cabinets create an arresting wall display in this monchrome scheme – they add to the decoration of the room and also provide useful storage.

The dining table is painted with a glossy white lacquer finish, and the wooden chairs that surround it were originally from an old school house. At a local wholesaler's tall stools in a similar style were found to use when sitting at the higher surface of the island unit. All the seats, both old and new, were painted bright white to give a cohesive appearance. The island unit provides work space that can be used in conjunction with the kitchen as well as a breakfast bar.

The walls, the roof space, the beams and the dresser are also painted white, and the worktops are smoothly honed white marble flecked with grey markings. According to the owner, this durable work surface has withstood red wine spillages and hot pots without any ill effects.

The floor throughout is covered with thick white ceramic floor tiles and the splashback area is faced with finer white tiles laid in a diamond pattern. This change of direction for the wall tiles was done to break up the dominance of horizontal lines in the room, as seen on the table, the island unit, the cabinet doors and drawer fronts and the dresser. The unit doors are white painted wood and the base of the island unit is clad with wainscoting, also painted white.

Task lighting is provided by recessed spots in the beam over the island unit that light up the working area below, and by wall sconces beside the dresser, but the family prefers to dine by the more relaxing glow of candlelight, even at breakfast time, so a candelabra is often kept on the dining table.

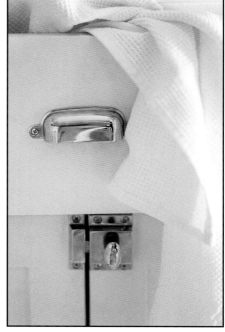

Furniture and decoration

The table and chairs have slim, pole-like legs and the table top is opaque glass, all of which helps to maintain the feeling of light and air (left). More solid furniture would reduce this effect. The decorative grouping of small mirrors is a pleasing feature of the scheme, but they also help reflect light as well as framing unusual reflections of the space.

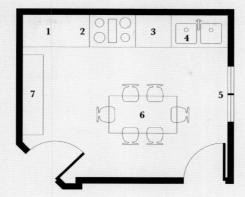

PLAN

1 Main area of worktop with small refrigerator underneath

2 Traditional-style cooker and hob with extractor fan

3 Dishwasher placed under the work surface but with exposed front

4 Twin sinks with single lever spout

5 Full-height double window

6 Utilitarian table and stackable chairs

7 Industrial metal shelving

MIX and match

To make the most of the limited space in this narrow kitchen the owner has kitted it out with a mix of fitted and unfitted furniture and equipment, some new, others old or second hand. This not only gives flexibility to work around difficult angles, but also creates a unique and characterful appearance that is difficult to achieve with a completely fitted and tailored kitchen made up of matching units. One tall set of open shelving provides a single block of storage for both foodstuffs and china. These shelves take up less space and light than conventional wall-mounted and floor cabinets.

Open shelving

This industrial-style metal shelving (below left) is widely available. Multi-adjustable, it comes in a wide range of shapes and sizes so it can be tailored to suit most wall areas and shapes. It can also be secured to the wall for a more stable fitting. But the items displayed on open shelving like this must be well maintained and interesting, as they are visually part of the design scheme.

Individuality

The view from the entrance hall into the kitchen (below) gives a taste of the quirky and unusual style to come.

This mix-and-match room contains all the usual components of a kitchen – a double ceramic sink, a cooker and various other appliances – yet they do not dominate the room because they are all concentrated below eye level. The kitchen function is almost a secondary aspect in the room because the colour scheme, the collection of unusual decorative objects and the lack of any conventional cabinet storage make it feel less like a working area and more of a casual dining, relaxing room.

THE USE OF SPACE

These days space is a precious commodity so make the most of what you have by keeping clutter to a minimum and by using decorative and architectural techniques to help you find more space.

Decoration can enhance the feeling of airiness in a room and might also give the impression that there is more space than there really is. White walls and ceiling and pale-coloured flooring is the most obvious choice, but panels of colour can also be successful. Vivid and bright colours, such as yellow, blue and pale green, can make a small dark room appear brighter, but beware of doing all the walls in the same colour as this can make the space seem smaller and claustrophobic. Painting just one wall or a panel of colour can be enough.

Instead they appear to float, especially at night if strip lights are used on top and under the unit. This is the opposite of the fully fitted kitchen, which fills in every inch of space to make a room feel full and enclosed.

Another decorating trick is to lead the eye through or past confined areas to spacious vistas beyond; the view could be into another room or out of the window to a garden. Light can also exaggerate space. An up-lighter in the floor can be focused to shine up the wall to emphasize height and lights around the perimeter of a space will make it feel wider.

There are often architectural solutions to the search for space: a glass extension, for example; or glass insets or panels in a roof; or the removal of internal walls to join rooms together or to create an extra external passageway into a room. A popular effect that is often employed by architects and interiors designers is to raise cabinets off the ground and to leave what appears to be a gap. This effective technique is also employed between the top of the upper wall units and the ceiling, an arrangement that prevents the units from appearing too solid and boxy.

Clutter is the enemy of space and where things accumulate in piles and stacks you are denying space its existence. But, at the other extreme, a room devoid of any visual stimulus will appear clinical and boring, so a compromise must be found. Try to select items to be on show on the basis they are there for a purpose, whether to display their intrinsic beauty or because they are useful. Make sure that such unnecessary things as discarded jackets, or piles of unopened mail and magazines, for which a family kitchen is often a magnet, are dealt with elsewhere.

The library
The broad shelves (left), reached by the steel ladder, house an extensive book collection. The generous platform area at the base allows you to sit and browse comfortably as you search for the right book. The steel ladder with its stabilizing hook-catches on the top (right) was custom made, as was the steel worktop in the kitchen section.

Open kitchen
When the sliding doors are open the main part of this compact but well-equipped kitchen is fully accessible. (far right). Other machines, such as the refrigerators and the central-heating boiler, which are needed less often, are placed in the separate end sections (below right).

CONCEALED cuisine

This apartment is in a 17th-century building, so when asked to provide a kitchen and library, the architects were reluctant to interfere with the original layout and fabric of the rooms. They avoided building internal walls and chose instead to accommodate the functions in an unusual mezzanine arrangement. The height of the room allowed for the library to be contained on an upper level, retaining enough head height below to configure the kitchen in four recesses concealed behind a wall of sliding oak doors.

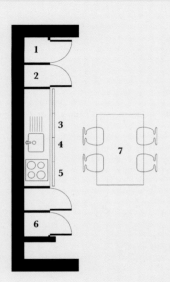

The functions of the kitchen have been separated so that they are grouped in their own recesses. In the section nearest the front door is a coat cupboard and general hanging and storage space. At the other end of the room, by the windows, is the section that contains the washing machine and the central heating boiler. The two centre recesses accommodate the refrigerator and wine fridge to the left and, on the right, the main workstation.

The workstation has a steel work surface inset with an induction-system hob, an oven, sink and dishwasher. In small wall-mounted cupboards above there is some storage as well as under-unit lighting. When not in use the doors can be slid right across and the kitchen functions are concealed. A table and stools placed in front of the doors also have a double life – they can be used for dining or for reading and studying books from the library above.

The floor, made in fine white sand cement, has been surface treated to have a wood-grain appearance complementary to the large door panels, which have been sealed with a matt varnish which protects, but does not conceal, the grain of the wood.

OPENING UP the space

The brief for this kitchen was for a scheme that did not make it look too obviously like a kitchen, because it is in a link location between two rooms. An initial worry was this internal space might be dark, especially when the double doors to the formal dining area were closed, but the glass extension in the breakfast room helps keep light levels up, as do the reflective fascias of the units – surfaces that are handsome but hardwearing enough to cope with the everyday needs of a family with four young children.

Linking rooms

This kitchen is in a wide corridor location between the breakfast room, with its adjacent living area (right), and the formal dining room at the far end (below). The doors to the dining room are generally left open, so the kitchen is on view from both sides and natural light flows into this inner space.

Family dining

A round table and curved Arne Jacobsen chairs (right) relieve yet complement the linear design of the kitchen.

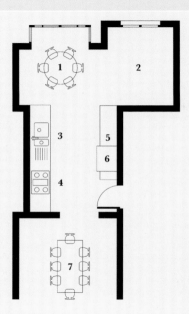

PLAN

1 Informal dining area and breakfast room
2 Family room and casual living space
3 Double sinks recessed below worktop
4 Raised gas hob
5 Wall-mounted ovens
6 Recessed fridge-freezer set into storage unit
7 Extendable oblong table in formal dining area

The cooker and refrigerator are placed on the opposite wall. Although this is essentially a corridor, it is not as narrow as a true galley kitchen and there is space on either side for people to pass through to the other rooms.

This corridor location of the kitchen is crucial in this series of interlinking spaces; the proximity of both the formal and family dining tables and the near-by living space to the kitchen means adults and children, or

hosts and guests, can occupy adjacent but easily contactable spaces.

To comply with the client's brief for a 'non-kitchen looking' kitchen, the designer used louvered aluminium shutter-style doors on the upper units. Although there are several small cupboards in the run, you really only register them as one complete cabinet because your eye is visually led along the continuous lines on the surface; the individual cupboards are only revealed when their doors are opened. These units are also completely handle free and they open upwards rather than outwards.

Work surface
The Ubatuba stone worktop was continued a part of the way up the wall to form a small return that reduces the expanse of steel splashback (above).

Adjacent living space
The seating area is next to the breakfast room (above right). Accessible from the kitchen, it is part of the family-oriented design of the house.

Much has been made of the basic principle of designing a kitchen around the famous work triangle, but in linear kitchens such as this the layout simply cannot accommodate it. Instead, the functions are arranged in a parallell scheme. The hob and sink with an area of work surface are on one side, with wide drawers for storing heavy pots and

pans located directly under the hob. The

The dark Ubatuba stone work surface was chosen primarily because it is hard wearing, but also because it has a subtle brown fleck that complements the rich colouring of the Panga Panga wood flooring. To lift what might otherwise become a dark scheme, the lower cupboard doors are finished with a high-gloss polyester surface that is easy to wipe clean, so child friendly. These floor cabinets do have handles, but they run the full width of the doors, which complements the lines of the shutter doors above. They are in a subtle aluminium finish that is not only aesthetically satisfying, but also very practical because it is easy to maintain.

A length of shelf was fixed to the area of splashback between the upper units and the worktop to break up the space and also to further emphasize the horizontal lines of the design, and the extractor fan above the hob has been concealed beneath another section of the shutter panelling.

DOORS AND OPENINGS

The upward-opening doors on the wall cupboards in this kitchen are not only visually attractive, they are also practical. They are fitted with a regulated hinge mechanism that allows a door to be partially opened and to be held in position at any height. Other less complex hinges only allow for the door to be locked in the fully raised position or to be hand held in the mid position, so you do not have both hands free to lift out items from the shelves.

This upward-opening feature is also useful because it doesn't take up too much crucial working space. Sideways-opening doors might clash, opening door over door in the same space, and leave pointed corners in a dangerous position over the worktop. By lifting the doors upwards the sharp corners are generally raised above head height. In confined spaces sliding doors that open across each other, or even fabric panels instead, can also save valuable inches.

LIGHT appeal

The rear of this small terraced house had previously been extended to include a dark, lean-to style kitchen with a bathroom in the adjacent room. The footprint of the building remained the same but the construction was reconfigured and largely re-built to create a light kitchen with a doorway opening onto the garden and an extended outdoor food preparation and eating area. The dining room was linked to the kitchen by two openings, with French doors in the end wall giving further access to the garden.

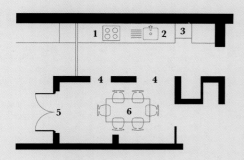

PLAN

1 Cooker and hob with low canopied vent
2 Single oblong countersunk sink
3 Stacked run of cantilevered shelves
4 Openings from dining area to kitchen knocked though original outside wall
5 Double French doors to garden
6 Linear dining room with view of garden

Stunning aspect
The bright purple-blue wall in the kitchen (left) brings a striking panel of colour and an upbeat aspect to a room that is essentially linear, with angular fittings and industrial surfaces.

Bringing in the garden
The limestone work surface of the main kitchen is extended beyond the glass window and into the garden (right), where it can be used for al fresco entertaining. The continuation of this visual line also makes the kitchen appear longer and an integral part of the space beyond.

THE CASEBOOK

The roof of the rebuilt kitchen is formed from a metal structure into which pre-formed, double glazed, sealed units of toughened glass with thermal reflective properties were inserted. The vertical panels that form both the rear window and hinged doorway are based on a 1930s industrial design, which was custom made for this project.

The substantial worktops are limestone, which is durable and will not fade or be affected by the high levels of heat and light in this area, and the flooring in both the kitchen and dining area is made of concrete paving slabs, the type usually specified for external use. Exposed shelving, including the 'flying' shelves, is all stainless steel, and the doors of the lower, fitted base cabinets are made from surface-treated MDF.

The lighting circuit was purpose made for the location, and in the kitchen consists of several 'layers' of illumination, including some directional spots and a wall-mounted, nautical-style enclosed circular fitting. In the dining area there is a variety of lights, some on dimmer controls, so that the mood and strength of the lighting can be varied.

The space is warm and light in summer, but in winter additional heat is necessary, so there are tall, pillar-like radiators in the recesses of the archway leading from the living area. The reflective glass directs heat and light away during summer, but in winter it insulates and holds heat within the room.

COLOUR

Instead of decorative tiles or painted units a single wall of vibrant colour can be enough to influence the appearance of a whole room. This home owner's brief to his arctitect was to create kitchen and dining areas with a simple, almost monastic feel. But to alleviate the neutral scheme and hard surfaces of his kitchen he introduced large areas of vivid blue. The shade was selected by the client from a photograph of a teapot found in a magazine, and matched exactly to create the paint.

When choosing a feature colour, you should test it in both day and artificial light to see how the colour responds. This particular shade has an element of red in its composition, which makes it warm, whereas white-based shades can appear cold.

FEATURE SHELVING

These cantilevered shelves appear to fly from the wall but are in fact fixed by rods that run through the length of the internal structure. The outer casings are stainless steel, which makes them easy to clean, important in an open kitchen where steam and grease will collect.

Introducing light

The tall narrow openings from the back of the house into the kitchen and dining areas (far left) are echoed in the side accesses from the dining room to the kitchen. This uniformity of simple style and shape prevents the four openings from becoming a muddle of doorways, and it creates pillar-like blocks of wall that help to maintain the enclosed separate aspect of the dining space. The four openings from the kitchen also allow generous amounts of natural light to spread from the glazed area into the darker, internal rooms.

A **MOVABLE** feast

To make the most flexible use of this spacious open room the owners devised a movable island system. The units, which are raised on locking wheels, are made up of two connecting sections that are used in a variety of ways to serve different functions. On a day-to-day basis, the units are locked together in the kitchen area. For parties, they are pushed back to the side, out of way of the main flow of space, and for dining they are placed parallel to the table to form a side table from which to serve.

Display cases
The decorative detailing of the cut-out recesses in the mobile unit is mirrored by four similar-sized openings in the wall behind (below left). These display areas are designed to be a feature in their own right.

The custom-made island is constructed from MDF, as are the wall-mounted units, and all have been spray painted with a white lacquer finish. The worktop of the mobile unit is in the same maple wood as the floor. The flooring, in extra-wide hardwood boards, has been sealed with a high gloss two-part acrylic lacquer.

The cut-out recesses on the front of the units are used as a display area and house vases or small groups of objects, rather than piles of clutter. This discipline is in keeping with the linear and minimal overall appearance of the room, but the colourful linings of the spaces prevent the scheme from being clinical. On the other side there are spacious cupboards, which contain cookery books and pots and pans.

By using a flexible cable, which plugs into floor sockets with protective covers, electrical goods such as a kettle, juicer and toaster can be used on top of the unit.

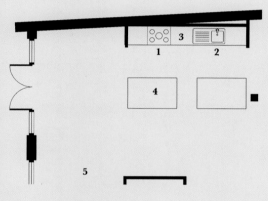

PLAN
1 Freestanding double oven and integral hob
2 Single sink and drainer
3 Main run of unified work surface
4 Two-part mobile island unit
5 Formal dining area

Defining light
The row of three ceiling-hung lights (below left) does impart some illumination, but it is mainly a decorative feature, defining the unit in its usual everyday location, parallel to the fixed work area and oven. Other, more direct, utility lighting is provided by under-unit fittings and daylight comes from the tall floor-to-ceiling windows.

Ultimate flexibility
To provide extra work surface close to the cooker, one of the units is moved to an alternative position (below), at right angles to the wall units. The front and the sides of the unit are raised to hide food preparation from view from diners.

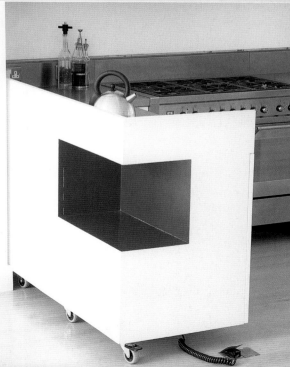

THE COOK'S KITCHEN

People who really enjoy cooking take pleasure in spending time in their kitchen; to them it is a place of adventure and alchemy. The enthusiastic cook invests time in planning and makes the best of every aspect of the room.

Brilliant meals have been produced over a single gas ring and with just a couple of pots and pans, but in the day-to-day scheme of things most keen cooks set about their tasks in a kitchen – it doesn't have to be a vast space but it should be a well-planned one to make the experience of creating a meal an efficient and enjoyable one.

Some cooks like to be part of the interaction and conversation that goes on between a couple, a family or dinner guests while a meal is being prepared and to accommodate this they often have kitchens that

Keen cooks might also enjoy a particular style of specialist cuisine – Oriental, griddle cooking or Tepanyaki style, for example. This different type of cooking may require a specific type of equipment so that instead of a four-ring hob, a double burner with an adjacent hot plate will be more appropriate, and for someone keen on rice and noodles a wall-mounted steamer may be more useful than a microwave.

Surfaces are important in a cook's kitchen because they will have to withstand plenty of use and subsequently plenty of vigorous cleaning.

are part of a bigger room that includes the dining area. Or they include a breakfast bar area where people can sit on a stool and chat over a cup of tea or a glass of wine and observe the culinary action.

Other cooks dislike distraction and will keep the kitchen separate from the living or dining room. Friends and family may be entertained in a separate sitting room and only allowed into the kitchen/dining room when the meal is ready to eat. So when designing or deciding on the location of a kitchen be clear what type of cook you are.

Someone who enjoys making pastry from scratch will appreciate a cold marble worktop to roll it out on, and a chef who routinely prepares fish or joints of meal will benefit from a similar type of surface. Cool and chill storage for fresh ingredients will be vital, dictating a large refrigerator, as will small shelves or brackets for containing condiments and spices. Enthusiasts will also have a battery of good sharp knives, in different sizes and thicknesses to perform various tasks; these will need to be carefully stored so as not to leave the sharp blade exposed.

Heavy-duty cooker
The duel-fuel range (left) is set against the substantial splashback of stainless steel and under a hood housing an effective extractor fan. Down-lighting illuminates the work surfaces below. Adequate ventilation and extraction are crucial when you use professional-style equipment because high levels of condensation and heat are created.

THE SERIOUS chef

This kitchen is the domain of a couple who both really enjoy cooking and entertaining – they wanted a hard-working space that included some serious heavy-duty equipment to provide a variety of cooking options. Their period house has listed status, so they have created a large flexible open space without altering the fabric of the building. The room has been cleverly configured to meet the requirements of a busy, productive kitchen and an attractive and appealing dining space.

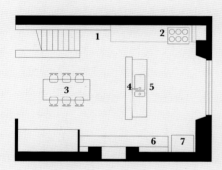

PLAN
1 Grill recessed in old chimney hearth
2 Professional-style oven and gas hob
3 Separate but linked dining area
4 Central work unit with raised front panel
5 Stainless-steel sink
6 Open shelving
7 Freestanding refrigerator

Wood-burning grill
The original fireplace was reconfigured to provide an open wood-burning oven, ideal for indoor barbeques and Mediterranean-style cookery (left). The area in front was faced with Acero stone to withstand sparks and the heat of the red-hot embers, and to look good.

Central workstation
The low freestanding wall in front of the large window (above) conceals a working area and the custom-made steel sink. Because the unit is low and it is designed to echo the proportions of the window it does not obstruct much of the flow of natural light streaming in.

51

Functional units
The low-level freestanding walls (below) contain the kitchen and provide a functional working area, but do not restrict or limit access to the rest of the room. The angular box-like shapes are echoed in other units and casings in the room.

Cabinet doors
Flat, featureless doors (right) keep the impact of the units to a minimum; their simple shapes and clean lines complement the rest of the room.

Open storage
Display is a feature in this kitchen, not only in open shelves (far right), but also in the niches and panels (below and right) that complement the wood-fired grill, another geometric shape in the wall.

To establish an efficient working space the kitchen was divided into three individual counter units. The first is a centrally located, custom-made cabinet that houses a stainless steel double sink unit with a steel splashback, a single lever water control and a moveable spout, plus a preparation area that is concealed behind a half wall. This screening wall keeps the pots and pans and other unattractive working aspects of the kitchen hidden from view, but allows the cook to maintain contact with friends and guests in the rest of the room.

The second counter is based around the original fireplace, which was adapted to contain a wood-burning oven and grill. The Acero stone counter acts as a hearth as well as a work surface and the inner walls of the hearth have been fitted with brackets which allow the grill to be moved up and down over the glowing embers.

The third counter area is focused on the large Thermador duel-fuel cooking range with its stainless-steel finish and extensive steel splashback area. Over the range is a custom-made canopy containing the vent and the task lighting, which focuses on the grill and the surface of the range as well as the adjacent worktop.

An imposing freestanding Sub Zero refrigerator with a large enough capacity for a busy kitchen stands in the corner to act as a piece of furniture in its own right. Open shelves allow certain pieces of crockery, china and cooking vessels to be left out on display and featureless drawers and panel-fronted units contain the rest.

The lighting needs are supplied in four different ways for absolute versatility. There is a certain amount of natural light from the window that dominates the space. This is supplemented by recessed low-voltage down-lighters set over the work surfaces; warm-toned white fluorescent strip lights in all the niches and gaps; and wall-mounted tungsten halogen up-lighters that use the high white ceiling as a diffusing surface.

Although the style of this kitchen is clean, contemporary and for serious cooks, the floor is traditional and domestic in feel; salvaged oak boards ware laid in a herring-bone pattern and waxed to maintain the aged appearance. This flooring and the original sash window are in keeping with the period style of this listed house. The paint finishes and colours are in a range of off-white shades specified by the architect.

STAINLESS STEEL

This is a practical surface because it can withstand high temperatures and is long lasting. Steel features in all professional kitchens because it can be hygienically washed down with boiling water. It does scratch, and on a highly polished surface these are obtrusive, but on softer more matt finishes these marks just become part of the overall effect. Stainless steel is easily marked by abrasive cleaners and wire cleaning pads, so to maintain a good steel surface use only a soft cloth and recommended cream cleaners.

COOKING for the family

The kitchen of this family home was small and dark, and tended to be used only as a place in which to cook, rather than as a social or family room. To overcome this, the existing room was gutted and the back wall removed. The kitchen was extended by the addition of a conservatory, which added natural light and gave a free flow of space. And, crucially, a hotplate was incorporated into the central counter. Family and friends can now enjoy watching food being cooked and take an active part in its preparation.

Seating
Comfortably padded metal stools with foot rails and lower back supports (below) provide seating around the island unit. The bright red of the upholstered leather seats adds a splash of colour.

The kitchen has the conventional cooking faciltes of hob and wall mounted oven, but also features a tepanyaki griddle. This electrically heated, circular hotplate is set into the granite worktop, and when lightly oiled the hot metal surface provides a direct cooking surface. Although it is traditionally used in the preparations of Oriental specialities, this family also use it to cook more traditional and European dishes, such as eggs and tomatoes.

The island cooking station is also used for dining in conjunction with tall, comfortable stools. The family have found that cooking and eating around the hotplate has brought them together, as their young children can enjoy the visual spectacle and direct involvement of watching their food being cooked, rather than having the end product served to them in a separate room. The glazed addition to the kitchen, easily accessed through double doors, contains a secondary dining area, which can be used for more formal entertaining.

Tepanyaki cooking

The hotplate is set into a polished granite worktop (below) that can withstand the heat given off during cooking, as well as thorough and frequent cleaning. The dark surface also creates a frame around the steel disc, making a feature of it.

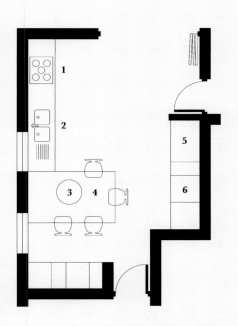

PLAN

1 Conventional hob inset into granite worktop

2 Counter-sunk double steel sinks

3 Steel disc tepanyaki grill

4 Island unit with overhanging edges for comfortable seating

5 Fridge-freezer with water chiller

6 Wall-mounted wall oven

Decoration

The decoration has been kept clean and classic (far left). Two walls are covered with floor-to-ceiling units faced with warm cherry-wood doors, which help to soften the contrasting and potentially stark black-and-white scheme elsewhere.

Ventilation

An extractor fan (left) is essential to absorb steam and smoke created when cooking on a hot plate.

FULLY functional style

This kitchen may be compact but there has been no compromise on style or on quality. The owner is a keen cook who likes to entertain; she specified certain pieces of equipment, such as the wall-mounted steam cooker, but also asked the designer to create for her a kitchen that would be an integral and glamorous part of her 1950s duplex apartment, and so the decorative theme shows some deference to this period.

Gadgets
The kitchen equipment is a mix of modern practicality, such as the steel fish kettle, (above) and period style, as well as a selection of ethnic-style ceramics. This vintage 1950s Cona coffee-maker (above left) subtly alludes to the period in which the apartment block was built.

Decoration
Rather than opt for simple low-key decoration, which would be safer in this small space (right), this designer has instead gone for impact. Black and white vertical stripes accentuate height in the room and the chequer-board mosaic floor offers geometric balance.

PLAN
1 Small steel-clad worktop
2 Professional-style oven and lidded hob
3 Single sink in front of window
4 Breakfast bar
5 Refrigerator

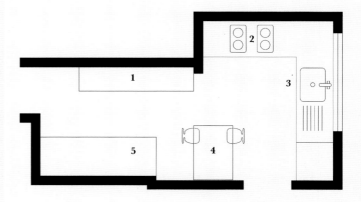

BREAKFAST BAR

A breakfast bar is an ideal place to take a snack meal or breakfast, or for friends to sit and chat over a cup of coffee. The surface of the bar does not have to be large; a small space can be adequate. The bar area can be raised as shown here (right) so it is set at a height that makes it more comfortable for a person to stand and work at when it is being used as a food preparation surface.

Allowing a section of the worktop to overhang is useful, because it enables people to pull their seats right up to the edge into a more comfortable position for eating when the bar is being used as a dining table. It can also prevent the surface below from becoming marked or soiled by any spillage that may occur during food preparation.

The two steel-framed Bertoia stools at the breakfast bar were designed by Harry Bertoia in the 1950s, and the two pendant lights hanging above have the vintage feel that echoes the period when the apartment was built. The polished steel surface can be cleared and used as an extra area of work surface when it is not being used for casual meals.

The apartment in which this kitchen in located is on two levels in a 1950s-built block. There are a number of small terraces placed around the exterior of the flat and the designer started with major internal reconstruction to give better access to these terraces, as well as to make the flow of the movement through the rooms more fluid and the overall decorative appearance of the flat a little more contemporary.

The owner, who lives alone, is a very keen cook and she specified that the kitchen, although small, should nevertheless be an interesting and tempting place to spend time in. But she was also adamant that these good looks should not compromise the serious business of cooking and the inclusion and use of specialist equipment.

In answer to these twin requests the designer eschewed the safe option of pale colours and plain surfaces and he chose instead to introduce a bold and decorative scheme. Using uncompromising black and white he had vertical stripes hand-painted onto most of the wall surface, an effect which creates a dramatic impact as soon as you open the door to this room. But this bold stripe has been used cleverly and in moderation. Opposite the window and sink area the wall is plain white, which reflects the available natural light and prevents the small room from becoming too box like and claustrophobic. Large panels of reflective splashback also help to increase a feeling of light and spaciousness.

The stark black and white scheme is also softened and warmed by purpose-built cherry-wood cupboards and panels that surround the larger pieces of kitchen machinery, such as the refrigerator. The red element of the wood works well with the positive and negative colouring and adds an important natural component to balance the numerous steel machines and handles.

Flooring

The chequerboard flooring (below left) is made from aged black-and-white mosaic tiles. Instead of using individual larger solid black and solid white tiles, which would have competed with the strong linear pattern on the walls, the designer selected this softer, less dominant arrangement.

Surfaces

A stainless-steel splashback incorporating window panels is located behind the pre-formed steel sink and worktop (left) for targeted illumination in this key working area within the kitchen.

Specialized machines

Certain key pieces of equipment, such as this wall-mounted steamer (below), were specified by the owner, who is a very keen cook.

The floor, laid in a chequerboard pattern, is made from aged black-and-white marble mosaic tiles. The strongly graphic wall-mounted and ceiling pendant light fittings were selected to reflect the 1950s heritage of the building. They are also interesting in that they break up sections of the wall's vertical stripes with their horizontal design. Light panels set into the splashback offer equally strong linear shapes.

ANCIENT and modern

The part-cottage, part-barn construction of this early 19th-century country house dictated the way this kitchen would be laid out. The old inglenook fireplace dominates one wall; another is taken up with a window and a third with the door and access to the room beyond, so there is a lack of wall space on which to place cupboards and equipment. But the owner has not allowed the demands of the space to compromise her choice of a modern professional cooker to meet the needs of a busy family kitchen.

Apart from the lack of wall space in this kitchen, none of the walls is straight, so the fitting of regular cabinets would have been difficult. Instead the owner opted to have the furniture custom made for the room and moved most of the food storage to an adjacent pantry. The main piece of furniture is a long table made with a stainless-steel frame and a solid oak top; it is fitted with drawers accessed from the side closest to the oven. The table is tall, which makes it a good height to work at, but it is also used as a dining table for informal meals. Tall stools supply the seating on one side and solid wooden block stools, which echo the thick wooden beam over the fireplace, are found on the other side. They neatly slot in under the table when not in use.

The floor, which is made of reclaimed York stone, is sympathetic to the surround of the inglenook. A modern adjustable light rig hangs over the centre of the table.

Freestanding style
The deep recessed fireplace easily accommodates the huge cooker, a work table and a flip-top bin (left). This arrangement of machinery and other equipment is in keeping with the non-fitted appearance of the room.

Plumbing
The working funtions have been concentrated around the fireplace. The double sink (below) is recessed into another custom-made unit, which is faced in stainless steel and also contains the modern dishwasher.

Old meets new
Uncompromising shelving, and industrial stainless-steel finishes (right) contribute to the modern business-like appearance of this rustic kitchen, without detracting at all from the character of the original features.

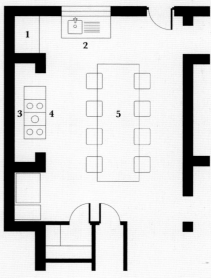

PLAN
1 Industrial-style open metal shelving
2 Sink unit incorporating the dishwasher, positioned in front of the window
3 Original farmhouse fireplace
4 Professional steel-clad cooker
5 Custom-built island work unit

DEALING WITH SIZE

Size matters, especially when it comes to planning and designing a kitchen. In most cases we feel we need more space, but in a few daunting cases, we have too much. How do you tackle this dilemma?

This chapter is about working within the physical constaints of your home to find out the most appropriate size of kitchen and equipment to suit your needs. A big kitchen is not necessarily best – in some cases a small one is more effective and less demanding that an outsized one.

With a large kitchen you need to focus attention, to create rooms within the room. This can be done with a nominal wall or low partitions which define an area without cutting it off. In a kitchen this is often done by incorporating an island unit or a breakfast bar. This linear structure will

In a small kitchen it may be that what you have to do is remove certain secondary tasks from the room, so that the main core functions of food preparation and cooking can be accommodated more comfortably. For example, washing machine and laundry facilities could be plumbed into a bathroom, hallway or cloakroom. A refrigerator and freezer could be put in a lobby, boxed in or disguised behind a curtain or screen so that it is not an eyesore. In small rooms the size of equipment and furniture really matters and it could be worth looking at scaled-down models,

not only provide a parallel work area, but will also help identify the work zone or cooking area of the kitchen. On the far side of the unit or bar you may place high stools, which signify that this is an area in which you and your friends and family can sit down and relax. If the room is large then a separate dining table and more formal chairs may be arranged to provide another facet to the room's use, and if larger still there may be a sofa or easy chairs, television and a family space where children can play while still being supervised by a parent in the kitchen.

even items designed for use in trailers, caravans, boats and motor homes. These vehicles generally have open-plan living and sleeping areas yet they manage to incorporate a fully functioning kitchen, usually neatly concealed behind doors and shutters. In a spacious kitchen you can afford to be generous with the furniture, but when size is on the lower end of the scale foldaway and dual-purpose items and equipment can be a benefit. But whatever your situation – if your kitchen is too small or too large – there is always an ideal way to configure the space.

A DECORATIVE approach

There was an option with this kitchen to make two smaller spaces into one large one, but it was decided to keep the areas separate and have a kitchen that is solely for cooking and eating and a laundry room that also provides ample storage. There are sliding doors between the two spaces so that they can be separate or linked. In the kitchen, the main work surface has a curved façade that plays off the peak design of the wall unit opposite, from which the table is cantilevered. These curved pieces of furniture give a softer look to the room and maximize the available space.

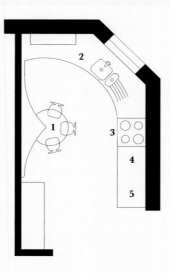

PLAN
1 Custom-built circular table with Pyrolave top to match work surfaces
2 Curved section of work surface
3 Surface-mounted hob
4 Wall-mounted oven set into matching wooden-faced cabinets
5 Fridge-freezer with matching wood veneer fascia

Individual styling
Vibrant colours make this an enjoyable room to be in and custom-made fittings such as the elm-wood plate rack and glass shelf bring personal touches (left). The plates add pattern on a plain wall and offset the angular harlequin motif.

The worktop
The smooth, curved shape of the Pyrolave work surface (right) makes it easy to work close up, as there are no hard angles, and its hard shiny top is simple to wipe clean. The Pyrolave base is made from a natural, lava rock that can be finished in a range of colours. It is shock and scratch resistant and impermeable to flames, water and grease.

THE CASEBOOK

By dedicating the kitchen space to the core activities of cooking and eating, and using the adjacent space as a laundry, there is scope to vary the decoration. The laundry and pantry are more simply finished with a sunny yellow scheme, but every ounce of space has been used to accommodate not only dried and tinned food storage but also items to be recycled and supplies of bottled water as well as the equipment needed for washing, drying and ironing clothes.

The kitchen, freed of these mundane requirements, is given a more decorative and colourful scheme, the single most vibrant item in the room being the lime green, custom-made Pyrolave worktop that curves over the units in front of the window.

The sweeping curve of the worktop is carried through to the cupboards, which have been kept plain, with the exception of a painted groove that continues and emphasizes the line of the curve. The doors are finished with an attractive light-coloured ripple sycamore veneer. The curved shape gives added interest and a more useable work area in this small kitchen.

The floor is covered with sturdy yellow ceramic tiles, specifically made to withstand the pressures of floor use and the splash-backs around the worktop and behind the hob are made from panels of Putsch glass.

THE USE OF COLOUR

This colourful scheme is united by the strength of colour used and the fact that the colours all appear together in nature – think of flowers such as irises. Also, yellow is a component colour of green and green and purple share a common base of blue, so there is a common base between them. When choosing colours try to focus on two or three main ones and then look at lighter or darker shades that come on either side, for example those with a little more white or black in their composition. These lighter and darker shades can be used to highlight and emphasize the main colour.

The kitchen area is compact, so everything needed for food preparation is easily within reach. The cantilevered table, also made of Pyrolave in distinctive lime green, provides useful additional work space. There isn't a great deal of natural light available through the window, but what there is amplified by the light bright colours that have been used in the decorative scheme.

With a small space you need to be aware that the pattern and design element of the scheme is not too large or overpowering. Here the diamond harlequin motif has been used sparingly, in fine line relief at eye-level on the cabinets, and in a denser pattern on the front of the peaked table cupboard. This subtle use of pattern enhances the whole room rather than dominating it.

An extra sink

A small square ceramic utility sink plumbed in the laundry room (below), is useful for soaking clothes, emptying buckets or arranging flowers
.

Doing the laundry

An old-fashioned pulley drying rack (above right) allows clothes to be aired. It can be pulled up high so that items are kept above head height. A neat stacking arrangement accommodates the washing machine and the tumble drier (right), rather than taking up limited lateral space.

Flooring

The staircase forms a subtle barrier to the breakfast bar and kitchen area (this page), but the same colour flooring is used throughout (with more pracical tiles in the kitchen area) so the space reads as one room.

Faking with mirrors

A single run of mirror-style splashback (right) creates the illusion of further depth in the room.

Multi-function

The first full-height cabinet (far right) is directly inside the front door to the flat, so this is used to hold coats and outdoor apparel rather than kitchen goods.

AN ILLUSION of space

This open-plan kitchen, on the ground floor of a small apartment, is in fact contained within an extremely compact area. But the clever use of light-reflective materials has created a feeling of height and spaciousness. The lower cabinets have been tailored in a slight curve in front of a window and have a high-gloss paint finish to bounce off all available light; whereas the upper wall-mounted units have frosted glass doors – they create an open, less dominant appearance without the distractions of open shelving.

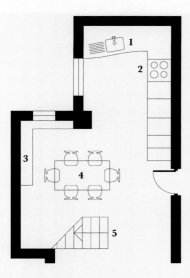

PLAN

1 Sink, slightly offset in the curved section of worktop
2 Single oven and surface-mounted hob
3 Raised breakfast bar
4 More formal dining area
5 Staircase to upper floor with transparent re-inforced glass and metal sides

The small kitchen has a tailored breakfast bar area set in beside the glass and steel staircase. The open construction allows for an unobstructed view and for light to pass through from one side of the room to the other, but creates a partial barrier between the living and the cooking sections.

The standard MDF cabinet doors were given an expensive-looking appearance by spraying them with motorbike paint in an unusual shade; aerosol paint designed for vehicles creates a hard, resilient finish.

A SUITE of rooms

The owners of this newly built house wanted their kitchen to combine many functions – a serious cook's kitchen with an entertaining space, as well as an area for the family to watch television and relax – and had the space in which to achieve this. To accommodate all these requirements the kitchen was designed to have a pivotal role, between a window seating area and a lower-level sitting room. The central work unit, with its honed granite surface, has the appearance of a large refectory table from one side and this doubles as a dining bar.

Decoration

The décor has a traditional flavour but is not a pastiche; design elements such as the classic, carved legs on the island unit (far right) and the stained and bleached wood (below) soften the kitchen's industrial edge – the bank of refrigerators, a six-burner hob and griddle – and introduce a more traditional element. The limestone floor reflects the available natural light.

Lighting

A row of three oversized white lampshades create a design feature in their own right over the central unit (right), and they provide good illumination for the working and dining surface beneath. But a room of this size needs layers of lighting: there are also recessed spots in the ceiling, under-unit, hood and refrigerator lights as well as generous amounts of natural light.

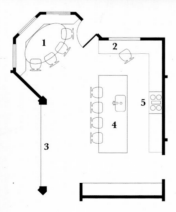

PLAN

1 Dining area with built-in bench seating in window
2 Area of work surface also used as a home office
3 Step to the lower-level informal family room
4 Table-style central island unit with carved legs
5 Professional-style cooker

HOME OFFICE

This spacious kitchen includes an area of home office, where a lap-top computer can be quickly plugged in and connected to a dedicated telephone line, so that household accounts or on-line shopping can be done easily. Ample storage is provided in a set of under-unit drawers, where the computer can also be stored when extra worktop area is needed for food preparation.

The priority for this series of interconnecting rooms was to create a family space; a location where meals could be prepared, cooked and eaten as part of a daily or evening routine involving all members, as well as friends, of the family. Allocating the proportions of the overall space was the first stage; this was done by creating a link between the rooms while retaining the individual use and character of each.

The decorative scheme was devised to be family orientated, unpretentious and casual, combining modern equipment and

Working space
On this side (left) the island unit conceals a waste bin, dishwasher, ice-maker and storage, all behind matching fascias. The passage between the sink, set into this unit, and the cooker on the wall side, is wide enough to allow doors and drawers to be opened but not so wide as to make it a journey.

More formal dining
An oval table with a built-in upholstered bench and chairs (above) is in an inviting spot in the bay window off the main kitchen.

DETAILING

The wall-mounted units are alternatively faced with solid wood and glass doors so only items worthy of display, such as neat stacks of matching white china, need be seen. These glass doors are echoed on the spacious commercial refrigerator, with its built-in chill drawers. Instead of being finished to the floor with a solid plinth, the refrigerator and tall wall units are raised on small feet, which add to the overall feeling of light and space.

features with subtle allusions to traditional detailing. Unneccessary embellishments have been kept to a minimum, leaving the quality and design to make a statement.

The sitting area is lower than the kitchen and so is reached by two long stone steps. This feature creates a physical as well as visual break between the rooms and also enables anyone working in the kitchen to have a clear and unhindered view of the room below, and so to feel included.

The dining area is behind a curving wall to one side of the lower area, but is barely visible from there, although directly linked to the kitchen. The windows of the bay also allow plenty of natural light to penetrate the inner, working section of the kitchen and give a pleasant view over the gardens.

The cook who uses this kitchen enjoys talking to friends and family while preparing a meal so the high stool area is used not only by the children at breakfast time but also as a bar area in the evening, or as a coffee perch during the day.

The palette of tones and colours used is muted and restful, and consistent with the schemes used in the rest of the house.

A **FAMILY** kitchen

This large kitchen is in a converted apartment on the top floor of an old industrial building situated close to a river. Some of the original features have been maintained and subtle hints to the waterside location are made with the occasional insets of vivid blue and the round porthole-style handles. The spacious family kitchen and dining space is separated from the sitting room beyond by a wall of doors, most of which conceal household machines and food storage. The long wooden beams that were part of the fabric of this historical building have been restored to form part of the decoration of this contemporary room, with industrial-style steel shelves fitted in between.

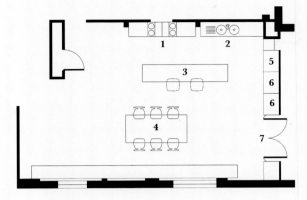

PLAN

1 Freestanding double oven and integral hob
2 Double steel sink
3 Island unit/breakfast bar
4 Extendable dining table in formal eating area
5 Double door refrigerator and freezer
6 Food and china storage cupboards
7 Matching double doors through to living space

Central unit

The steel-framed island bar has a display section facing the dining area (far left), but on the other side, facing the working kitchen, there are deep cupboards (below). Two classic Harry Bertoia model 420C stools provide informal seating.

Lighting

This room has good natural light. Additional lighting is provided over the table by pendant lights with Flos shades (far left). Recessed ceiling spotlights (below) focus on the surfaces below and under-shelf lighting is directed on to the areas of work surface by the wall.

Dividing doors

The end doors in the row of tall cupboards open to give access to the sitting room (left), but they can be closed to contain the kitchen and dining space (below).

SURFACES

The top of the custom-made steel island unit is finished with a length of synthetic resin. Heat resilient, yet warm to the touch, this material can usually be found in laboratory work stations, but it is also ideal for a kitchen work surface.

In contemporary kitchens, all types of materials can be used for work surfaces, as long as they can withstand heat, water, sharp blades and spillages such as oil, or acidic effects of liquids such as vinegar, wine and lemon juice.

This home was created by knocking two apartments together; the redesign was intended primarily to showcase the view and also to make the most of the available space. The owners were keen to maintain at least some of the features of the late 19th-century warehouse, such as the solid wood beams, but they also wanted a good-sized family kitchen that could accommodate more formal entertaining with family and friends.

The aim was to achieve an elegant but understated kitchen, with ample but mainly concealed storage. The clients specified the use of the strong blue colour on the base units of the island workstation and the

round porthole-style handles as an allusion to the waterside location of the building.

The open kitchen and dining area is partitioned from the sitting room beyond by a series of doors. A pair of double doors at the end open to reveal the room beyond, but the others conceal food storage and kitchen machines. In a narrow section, next to the refrigerator, a panel of glass has been used as an infill; this allows light from the stairwell in the sitting room to brighten up this far corner of the kitchen.

A stained oak floor runs throughout the apartment, uniting the various elements but also adding a richness and depth of colour that is appropriate to a building of this age.

The oak boards were initially dampened and then stained – the application of water loosens the grain and makes it easier for the stain to penetrate deep into the wood.

The custom-made steel-framed unit that divides the formal dining area from the kitchen proper is also used every day as a casual breakfast bar by the family. This tall unit is at a good height for food preparation and it forms part of the working triangle between the oven and the sink.

Glass infill
A panel of glass allows light from the stairwell behind into a dark corner (below). Wine glasses utilize the storage space, but do not block light.

Tiling
Subway-format tiles cover the back wall (left) to heighten the utilitarian feel. Artemide globe lights create a decorative but functional feature.

Plain detailing
The flat doors and the drawer fronts are simply painted (below left). The recessed porthole-like handles (bottom) refer to the river-side location.

ALL SEASONS AND EVENTS

These days, our kitchens are not just rooms where we provide sustenance for ourselves and family – increasingly they also need to be welcoming spaces where we can entertain our guests.

There are few things more frustrating when we are entertaining guests than to be stuck away from the action, sweating over a hot stove and emerging with various culinary offerings only to discover we've missed another punchline to a joke, or are listening to a particularly interesting piece of gossip, but have to disappear once again to rescue the main course. Whether you regularly give elaborate four-course dinner parties, will throw a party at the merest hint of a celebration, or keep an open house, happily supplying ad hoc meals for friends whenever they drop

some parties naturally seem to spill out from the house into the garden. When planning a new kitchen or alterations to an existing kitchen think through your annual dining routine and work out whether access to the garden, patio or yard would be useful. Try to analyse how often you eat outdoors and if you don't already do it, would you do it more often if it was easier to move people and paraphernalia outside?

To supply the food and drink for an outdoor celebration or event access from the kitchen should be as unhindered as possible. In many

by, your kitchen needs to be the focal point of your entertaining. After all, most socializing involves serving food of some kind, even if it is only party nibbles or catering-company cuisine that needs to be heated through, and it it far more fun to be able to enjoy the company of your guests while you prepare the food rather than be banished elsewhere.

Then there are the times of the year when we leave the dining table and shelter of four walls to eat outside – a rewarding move, because somehow food always seems to taste better when eaten outdoors. And

homes, French or double doors, or even sliding panels, can be opened up to link the kitchen to the space beyond. Although the garden may be an ideal place to sit and socialize, eat and drink, the cool of the house is usually the best place from which to serve food, and the nuisance of insects will be greatly reduced. For a large function, with a great many pre-prepared dishes you may need to have regular access to the kitchen and refrigerator, for topping up supplies when they run low, and cool drinks will stay icy for longer if they are kept inside before serving.

Light and airy
The kitchen and dining areas are divided by an island unit; on the kitchen side a small section of work surface and the sink are concealed from the diners' view. A series of metal-framed doors open out along the whole of the end wall to give easy access and excellent ventilation.

GARDEN kitchen

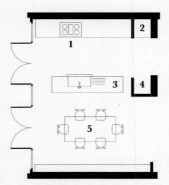

The original extension at the back of this house was demolished and replaced by a spacious new open-plan room incorporating a kitchen and dining space, but also making the most of the view and giving direct access to the garden beyond. Rather than make a completely glass structure, the architects and owner decided to create a more solid building, but to focus light on particular areas with overhead light wells.

Hidden from view
Looking from the garden into the kitchen (right) you can see how the sink has been recessed below the thick limestone worktop. A tall pillar-like unit has been constructed to provide the casings in which to slot white goods and machines, to keep them from view.

PLAN
1 Surface-mounted gas hob
2 Wall-mounted double oven
3 Central island unit with screened sink
4 Refrigerator contained in housing unit
5 Vintage zinc-top table

LETTING IN LIGHT

Although some people might have chosen to have a traditional conservatory-style extension, this well-devised scheme gives the client the best of both worlds. A room with glazed walls and roof would have allowed ample daylight in, but could have caused overheating, and problems with dazzling glare in summer, especially with the white-painted walls and pale surfaces. Here the walls and roof are solid, but a central light well has been positioned over the main area of worktop, mirroring it in size and shape. This, and the expanse of glass doors on the back wall, let in plenty of light and frame a wonderful view, but the walls give the room a more permanent and substantial feeling, and make it far more economical to heat and to use in winter. A smaller light well at the back of the room brings daylight in over the purpose-built recess that contains the oven.

Once the existing extension was removed from the back of the house, the rear wall was rebuilt so as to be flush. Two new large angular openings unlocked a narrow dark internal corridor and created a link running between the dining area on one side and the kitchen on the other.

In the new lower-ground floor extension the kitchen floor was lowered to increase the available head height and keep the level of the new roof line below the windows of the rooms on the floor above.

The pale sandstone floors that run throughout the lower-ground floor are under heated, which makes them comfortable to walk on in winter, but also allows the walls to be clear and uncluttered by radiators, adding to the simple unfussy appearance.

The pristine white walls are softened and made less clinical by a broad wooden shelf and solitary cupboard door panel in the kitchen, and a single display shelf in the dining area parallel to the sandstone work-top opposite, giving a pleasing balance.

The dining area is simply furnished with an antique zinc-top table, complete with graffiti acquired over the years, and six old wooden church chairs, with hymn-book holders at the back and padded cushions.

The simplicity and regular lines of the rooms focus the attention on the garden and the view beyond. In summer, the doors are opened, and the garden becomes an extra room in which to enjoy the pleasures of outdoor dining. In winter, the window is an ever-changing backdrop to the room.

Decoration
Although this kitchen room has been designed to be contemporary, the furniture and artefacts are old and some, such as the antique table and the utilitarian wicker baskets (above), are quite rustic. These soften the overall appearance and add to the feeling of comfort and domesticity.

DAY into night

A house built in the late 1800s was converted into apartments and the owners of this mid-level home chose a loft-style interior. They retained the original details and features of the main rooms, but incorporated a contemporary glass-panelled box to contain the kitchen. This created a semi-enclosed space for food preparation, but doors at either end allow for free access to the dining room to allow for interaction with guests when entertaining.

The box

When the single doors at either end are open (below), an aisle runs through the centre, connecting to the room beyond. The units on one side are fixed to the wall, but those opposite are freestanding. The top of the enclosure remains open, so the box does not interrupt the line of the architectural moulding on the original ceiling and it retains a free-floating quality.

Japanese style

The owners of the house lived in Japan for some time and that country's style influenced the appearance and finishes chosen for this project. The units are faced with a shiny black finish (right) inspired by Japanese lacquer work. The glass panels of the walls of the box incorporate a thin layer of Japanese-style paper (far right), which gives a muted, diffuse effect when back lit.

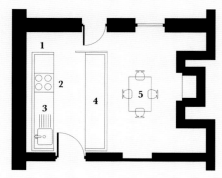

PLAN

1 Double-glass walls with a layer of Japanese paper form the shell of the box

2 Single oven and surface-mounted hob

3 Recessed sink set in a unit attached to the internal wall

4 Freestanding storage and work surface

5 Minimalist glass dining table and fabric-covered chairs

DEALING WITH SMALL SPACES

In a confined space like this, or in a kitchen open to a main living room, it is important to have effective extraction. Where ventilation is insufficient the limited space will become hot and steamy, and in a larger room the smell of cooking will soon permeate the whole space. The size and strength of the ventilation system will depend on the floor area and capacity of the kitchen, as well as the type of cooking you do regularly and type of hob or oven you choose.

Another issue is the limited room. In this kitchen the upper unit doors are on hinges that open upwards, giving clear access but not taking up any significant space.

The box is a sculptural but functional form that contains the working kitchen, but it is also a feature of the simply furnished room. During the day, internal lighting can be used for food preparation, but when not in use the lights can be turned off, making the box unobtrusive. At night time, when the box is internally lit by a series of halogen lights on dimmers, it becomes a significant feature.

The kitchen itself is compact and galley style but well thought out. The unit surfaces are kept simple and finished with a sleek combination of black lacquer and Hexalite.

Although it is black, the high-gloss surface reflects some light, so prevents the space from being too dark; if the surfaces were mat they would absorb light rather than increase it. The work surface is stainless steel made in one continuous run; the floor throughout is covered with fumed oak.

A powerful ventilation system takes moisture and cooking smells out of the enclosure and can be used in conjunction with the doors at either end, which open out on the far end opposite a set of French windows with access to a balcony.

Three levels of lighting – up-lighters, under-unit concealed fluorescents and halogen spots – provide good working light, but can be dimmed and varied to provide a moody, decorative glow when the box becomes a lighting feature rather than a work place.

Machines such as the dishwasher and refrigerator are covered with black lacquer fascias to make them blend with the other units and to maintain the minimal, unfussy appearance. The oven is set into a built-in casing and a ceramic hob is fitted into a custom-built stainless steel top.

A lighting feature
Here the kitchen box is shown in day time (above) without any additional artificial light, and then in the evening (right), when the internal up-lighters illuminate the translucent glass panels. The clear glass top and thin elegant metal frame of the table echo the beautiful construction of the box.

THE ENTERTAINING space

Industrial buildings, such as this disused factory, are often transformed into loft-style apartments with open-plan living areas. Here much of the original interior was gutted, but the style of the kitchen and dining area has been kept simple and basic, with industrial overtones that allude to the building's previous use. The kitchen is arranged across the width of the lower floor of the apartment and has two dining areas, a bar for up to four guests and a long table that can be erected in the centre of the room.

Cabinets
The units were constructed on a tight budget using standard carcases faced with routed and painted MDF doors (left). Open-shelf storage for china and glassware has been located in recesses at either end of the island unit, accessible for use on either the island or the main table.

Cooking
A four-ring burner with a griddle (right) is set into the island's ample Belgian Blue Stone work surface.

Dining
This view of the kitchen from the upper level (below) shows the overhang of the island unit, which provides a bar/dining site.

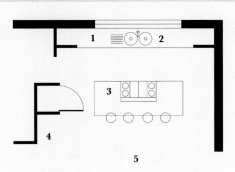

PLAN
1 Belgian Blue Stone work surface
2 Round stainless-steel sinks recessed into worktop
3 Island unit with hob and grill and overhanging unit to accommodate seating
4 Open-tread staircase to upper living area
5 Movable dining area with folding chairs and trestle table

THE CASEBOOK

Refrigerator
The large American refrigerator (right) was snugly recessed into the base of the stairs, within easy reach of the work area.

Artwork
The large walls can accommodate generously sized paintings (below and right).

Cantilevered staircase
The stairs lead past the red wall (bottom). The same oak is used for the stairs and for the flooring throughout the whole room.

When the upper two levels of this three-storey industrial building were bought for conversion most of the interior structures had to be removed but, having achieved an impressively large single open space, the owner decided to make the most of it.

Designed to be functional rather than fancy, the kitchen runs across the width of the room, leaving a clear open space in the centre. This can be used in various ways for entertaining; it offers a generous open space for a drinks party. Alternatively the custom-made trestle table can be set up; it is painted MDF on a metal base, 2.4m (8ft) long, with seating supplied by folding chairs that can be stored flat, when not in use, in a side cupboard. For smaller gatherings, the overhang of the island unit, with four adjustable-height stools, is used.

With hindsight, the owner says that the only thing he would change about this kitchen is this small dining area, because

This kitchen was fitted out inexpensively; the units are made from standard mass-produced carcasses but were given a very individual look with custom-made MDF doors. MDF is a cheap material that is very easy to work with, so it can be finished in a variety of ways to make it appear more luxurious, for example, painted wood graining or faux panels.

Sourcing local materials can help when you are working on a budget; you avoid high transportation costs. Work surfaces in this Brussels kitchen are Belgian Blue Stone, giving an agreeable regional aspect to the scheme.

people sit side by side in a long line rather than a cosy group. If he were doing it again he would not have the open shelving at one end of the island unit, so that stools could be drawn up there in a sociable L-shape.

Parallel to the island unit is another long run of Belgian Blue Stone worktop that contains two round steel sinks. Beneath the work surface there are rows of drawers and cupboards that supply ample storage space for pots, pans and comestibles.

Because the room is so sizeable it can accommodate large pieces of equipment, furniture and artwork. The steel-fronted refrigerator is a generously proportioned American larder-size fridge-freezer and the hob inset in the island unit has four rings and a griddle hot plate, over which is a powerful industrial-size extractor.

Large canvases of colourful artwork are easily accommodated in this impressive gallery; their vibrant hues and expansive

forms help to bring colour and pattern to the room, and bring a human scale to a space that could feel vast and intimidating.

Heating is supplied via large snake-like pipes that are left exposed, and again help to break up the expanse of bare wall space. Although three of the walls are painted plain white the fourth, where the staircase from the upper level is cantilevered from the wall, has been painted in a vibrant red that warms and again softens the room.

PLAN

1 French doors to deck and pool
2 Old-style freestanding cooker
3 Sink, recessed into Formica worktop
4 Upright fridge-freezer
5 Door to pantry
6 Small dining table
7 Painted cupboard that holds crockery and glass

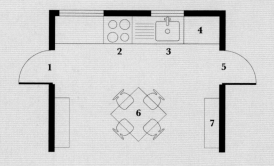

SUMMER entertaining

Kitchens can be fun places too. This 1950s holiday cottage has plenty of colour and panache and a limited amount of kitchen, but in summer this is used in conjunction with an outdoor deck and barbecue. Additional storage is supplied by a large painted cabinet, to the left of the French doors that lead out to the deck. This holds china and glassware and the laundry/pantry space beyond the kitchen, also linked to the deck area, is an ideal space for bulk storage and for keeping pre-prepared dishes cool.

Painted cabinet
The double-door cupboard (left) contains an array of china and glassware. It sits next to the pantry and the French doors to the deck, so the dishes it holds are easily accessible for indoor or outdoor use.

Table and chairs
The crisp and fresh red-and-white gingham check tablecloth and the hickory chairs (right) contribute to the light-hearted, holiday feel of the cottage. A small very informal dining area divides the kitchen from the main sitting area (far right).

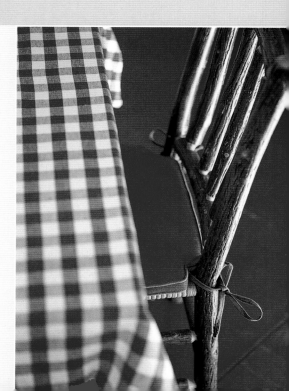

THE CASEBOOK

This small kitchen is part of a frequently used holiday home – it is a place where friends regularly come to stay during the summer and a retreat from the city in winter, so the emphasis on entertaining is very important. The accommodation comprises a porch to the front and a deck to the back with an open-plan living room. The kitchen itself occupies just one single wall, along which is cupboard storage, a small cooker, a sink and a large refrigerator. Because it is set to one side, there is a free flow of traffic through this central space and the kitchen is directly linked to, and accessible from, the deck and the pool area.

To keep in touch with the recreational purpose of the cottage, the chosen décor is bright and cheerful, and the individual style very much reflects the owner's love of vintage collectables. The floor throughout is wooden boards painted a bright red; this has an immediate impact on the overall scheme but is also very practical as it can be easily maintained and brushed clean of the sand and dust that is brought in from the deck and shoreline beyond.

The walls are also wooden, and these and the ceilings are painted plain white, which gives a light and airy feel, and which can be easily touched up or repainted as

Easy access
This view of the kitchen (above) is taken from the pantry and looks through, past the linear kitchen area, to the porch beyond.

Outdoor room
French doors link the dining and barbecue area on the outdoor deck to the kitchen inside (left). This area is decorated in the same characterful style as the indoor rooms, making the transition outdoors as comfortable and inviting as possible, so the space is used to its full advantage.

necessary. Echoing this construction, the row of kitchen floor cabinets have simple plank doors, again painted white, and they are finished with small red knobs. The top surface of the units is finished with a highly practical red laminate Formica, in keeping with the time in which the cottage was built.

Similar vintage road and shop signs to the ones displayed in the main room of the cottage are also used on the outside wall,

on the deck area, giving the impression that the outdoor dining area is linked to indoors. Much of tableware is enamel and the cloths and fabrics are old, giving a friendly patina of use and age, rather than being pristine perfect and hard-edge contemporary.

The layout, the colour scheme and the quirky accessories all add to the overall feeling of fun and enjoyment, which is what this holiday cottage is all about.

VINTAGE STYLE

If you have a particular theme or period style for your decoration you can accentuate it with accessories and fabrics. This home owner loves to browse in flea markets and junk shops, but he has a selective eye.

When looking for accessories, try to be guided by some unifying theme. Here, the owner has taken firstly the colours, the red-and-white décor of the main room, as a lead, then the 1950s pedigree of the house itself. He has also homed in on Americana, in deference to the location, but he is happy to blend new with old; for example, the new stars-and-stripes hi-ball glasses with a vintage Coca-Cola ice box. Finally, when selecting vintage and second-hand goods, always check the condition carefully, especially of any table and glassware – avoid anything that is chipped or cracked, and remember that older items may not be dishwasher proof.

95

Nuts and Bolts

INTRODUCTION

Fine tuning a kitchen scheme helps to unify the space and make it easy to use. When selecting decorative and utilitarian items research and test them, so that when you make your decisions you are well informed.

The planning and layout of your kitchen is fundamentally important, but the finishes and fixtures are equally significant – they contribute not only to the look, but also to the easy running and working of the kitchen. If the first phase is architectural work, then Nuts and Bolts is the next step, bringing the diverse functions – food preparation, washing, cooking, storage and dining – together in the kitchen and making them cohere in a single setting. These elements make a major contribution to the style and colour of the scheme and should be selected on their aesthetic

These days, with access to websites and an international address book of suppliers it has never been easier to track down machines and units, so you can explore every avenue. But, if buying from outside your home country, make sure the electrical and plumbing elements are compatible with the supplies, regulations and power sources available locally.

But kitchen fitting isn't just about selecting the right machines, it is also about meticulous forward planning to pre-empt any potentially disastrous situations. For example, you should look at the section on

merit as well as their suitability for your lifestyle and surroundings. Mixing and matching different machines, for example cookers with specialized functions such as steam cookers or hotplates, to achieve the perfect combination of functions is part of the 'trying and testing' process in the jigsaw puzzle analogy mentioned in the introduction to this book (see page 7). As machines are costly and need professional help to install, you should plan carefully to achieve the right combination for the size of your kitchen, as well as the quantity and type of food you prepare.

plumbing carefully (see pages 132–37) because most machines, such as dishwashers and even water inlets to chill units in refrigerators, need to have their final positions allocated early on in the planning stages so that the pipework and waste outlets can be provided for before the cabinets and the floor and wall surfaces are installed.

It is worth investing time and effort in this phase of kitchen design, because it is in the details that the quality and finish show through, and the sum of all these smaller parts will adds up to the final result.

SURFACES

Surfaces in kitchens can be divided into three areas: walls, floors and worktops. There are some materials that can be used on all three, but generally you need to choose specific finishes for appropriate properties. For example, ceramic tiles are easy to wipe clean on walls, but on worktops or floors (unless specifically made) they are liable to crack with constant use or break if heavy items are dropped on them. The grout can also become stained and unsightly.

Linoleum is a thoroughly practical surface for floors, but is not suitable near hot elements, as high temperatures can cause surface damage. Natural hard finishes, such as granite or marble, can be used on all three surfaces, but on the floor they may be cold to stand on for prolonged periods and require under-heating, and if used on a vertical surface they must be veneer thickness to avoid excess weight.

For all kitchen surfaces the priority is ease and efficiency of cleaning. Kitchens are steamy, greasy places, but hygiene is of utmost importance. Walls and worktops, where food or water may splash and spray, should be effortless to clean. Floors might also become oily or slippery, which is dangerous, so they must also be simple to sweep and to mop.

Below left: Reinforced safety glass is a durable and transparent surface, which will allow plenty of light to pass through it. The glass can be plain or frosted, or incorporate subtle patterns, such as this geometric one.

Below: In basement rooms maintaining the quality of light and of height is very important. In this kitchen neither is compromised; the glass splashback protects the wall but does not create a barrier or division.

Right: Louvered doors on the front of a row of wall cupboards encourage the eye to continue along the lines, so this façade appears as a single width rather than a number of small sections, echoing a granite worktop.

Bottom left: To facilitate cleaning, only items that are used frequently should be left on the main worktop surfaces and they should be stored in durable, easy-to-wash containers that have an attractive uniformity.

Bottom right: Durable surfaces, such as slate and mosaic tiles, have become increasingly popular in the kitchen because they can easily withstand heat, water and the use of sharp utensil points and blades.

Right: The back panel of this dresser has been lined with period-style wallpaper, which enhances the colour and patterns of the display of creamware arranged on shelves in front of it.

Below: White is a clean and light-reflective shade often used in kitchens, but there are various shades of white. Some include the warming elements of red or yellow, while others have a cooling blue tint. Check the paint colour in day and artificial light before application.

WALL COVERINGS

Wall areas can be subdivided. For the main part of the room a good-quality paint or a similar wipe-clean finish should be adequate, but in areas where the wall is in close proximity to a heavy-use section, such as the hob or main food-preparation worktop, a more resilient surface may be needed.

There are a number of surface finishes suitable for walls in the main part of the room. Gloss paint dries to a good, hard finish, but is not generally used on walls unless to achieve a lacquer or reflective effect. Vinyl paints dry to a washable, slightly shiny surface and are ideal for this sort of use. Vinyl wallpapers were developed with a washable vinyl resin or latex derivative coating, which not only makes them

wipable, but also prevents discoloration. But even vinyl papers are best kept away from the main steamy parts of the kitchen because the actual adhesive with which the paper is applied may eventually react with the moisture and cause the paper to peel.

Designated heavy-use areas are the splashback behind the sink, the wall behind the food preparation area on the worktop, and the gap between a hob or hot plate and an overhead extractor fan. Traditionally, these areas have been covered with ceramic tiles, but in recent times other materials have become popular. Solid panels of reinforced glass – opaque, sand-blasted, clear or the recently available ice finish – and polished or matt stainless steel or aluminium are favoured because they have no joins or recesses, making them easy to wipe. They are also low key, for minimal or understated kitchen designs.

Glass is generally easy to clean with preparatory solution or with a teaspoon of vinegar in warm water. The best way to retain a shine on a stainless-steel surface is to clean it with a recommended cream (never use wire wool or abrasive substances as they will cause fine starches), then polish it with baby oil and buff with a soft cloth. It is also worth noting that using too much steel in a kitchen can make it appear

cold and clinical, so mix it with materials such as wood, to give a softer more domestic appearance.

Rock and stone
These surfaces can be used in tile, sheet or panel form, but they are heavy and not generally cut in long single runs. Because of their overall weight, and expense, they tend to be used in smaller sections.

Man-made materials
Composite materials are manufactured from a mix of natural minerals and polyester or acrylic resins to form a non-porous, resilient surface that is waterproof and, in most cases, stain proof. Marks can be polished out with fine sandpaper if the surface is dented or scratched. Composites are manufactured in a wide variety of appearances, from 'fashion' colours such as lime or bright pink, to stone and wood effect.

Laminates
These surfaces are made from resin-impregnated papers fused under pressure at high temperatures. A clear, protective overlay is then applied before the facing is joined to a particle-wood backboard. The result is a relatively cheap and lightweight material. Laminates are available in many different colours and finishes, which include wood and granite designs that are almost indistinguishable from the real thing except by touch. There are also speckled designs, dotted and linear motifs and solid plain colours.

Glass
Glass makes a stunning surface finish: it has a light appearance, is reflective and it can be placed on top of coloured backgrounds to give an impression of gloss and depth. Interesting lighting features can also be used to make glass glow, whether a simple, small-scale strip light along one edge or a host of tiny fibre-optic lights that can be wired to a control panel that changes the colour. Toughened glass is the best type to use in the kitchen and it should be at least 15mm (⅝in) thick. Protect the surface from contact with hot pans and sharp blades because these can cause permanent damage, and glass should be frequently cleaned and polished to retain its good looks.

Wood
Although not often used as a splashback, wood can be found in kitchens walls as panelling, left natural or painted, and is frequently used as a worktop.

Metals
Stainless steel is now a standard splashback finish in kitchens; it is versatile and can be cut and formed into most shapes. Aluminium is increasingly popular and it can be finished with a brushed effect, which gives a soft, almost velvety appearance.

Below: This decorative concrete screed finish has a smooth, soft and mottled appearance, which belies its solid and durable qualities.

NUTS AND BOLTS

Below: This chequerboard flooring is made from aged tiles in a black and white mosaic. Rather than using large single tiles for the pattern, the designer chose to make up the geometric grid with small tiles, which created an appearance that is less stark and rigid .

Right: In this country-style kitchen, old-fashioned flag stones, or pavers, are laid to contrast the smooth and rough surfaces. They have been used to harmonize with the exposed brick work and beams found elsewhere in this room. In modern homes, this type of 'cold' stone floor is often under-heated for added comfort.

Below right: These square and hexagonal floor tiles were originally terracotta, but a soft colour wash was used to reduce the orange-ness of the tile and to link it more closely to the other colours in the room. Once the colourwash was dry, the surface was sealed.

FLOORING

Since flooring is usually among the final elements to be installed in a kitchen, many people think they can put off the decision as to which type to have. But you really should choose your floor at an early stage, in conjunction with the other materials in the room.

Ceramic tiles

These must be manufactured for floor use; don't try small wall tiles in this location or they will break. The shiny surface of glazed ceramic tiles is easy to clean and they come in a very wide variety of colours and patterns, but matt finishes are increasingly popular.

Slate, stone, limestone and marble

This type of flooring is generally expensive, but is an investment as it will last a lifetime. As these natural materials tend to be intrinsically cold many people opt for low-level under-floor heating to take the chill off the surface. This also has the advantage of freeing wall space that would otherwise be occupied by radiators. Slate tiles need to be sealed to form a waterproof top coat and will require regular maintenance. Marble can have a polished or matt finish, but if you do opt for a polished surface be aware that it might well become slippery with grease or water – you may choose to have mats of cork, cotton or some similarly absorbent material in the working areas by the sink and cooker. Make sure that any mats on these surfaces have a non-slip backing to avoid rucking and skidding.

Terrazzo, concrete and terracotta tiles

Terrazzo, made from concrete with chips of marble and stone, is an easy low-maintenance option, as is concrete itself, which can be finished with a sealant or rubberized coating. Terracotta is popular in traditional or rustic-style kitchens, but unless tiles are pre-glazed they will need to be sealed. For the most authentic finish, use boiled linseed oil and wax. Hand-made tiles have flaws and irregularities that are part of their character, but these irregular finishes have now been copied by manufacturers to give a hand-made look.

Above: Modern bricks can have an aged or reclaimed appearance and can create a useful and utilitarian floor in a rustic-themed scheme.

Right: You can break up the monotony of a large expanse of uniform paving with insets. Here a square of small mosaics has been set into a grid of pale stone tiles. Diamond shapes and contrasting colours can also be used to good effect.

105

Industrial rubber, linoleum, cork and acrylic

These surfaces are relatively inexpensive, and (except for acrylic) are made from mostly natural products such as latex, oilseed and bark. They are generally low maintenance and easy to clean; they are also warm and quiet underfoot, hygienic and non-allergenic. The disadvantage is that they are not as strong as stone or marble. The surface of linoleum may rip or scorch and cork will swell if inadequately sealed and exposed to water. The surface of cork will also singe or burn if brought in contact with a very hot pan or naked flame. But linoleum, industrial rubber and acrylic flooring can all be bought off the roll and, depending on the size of the area, can be laid in a single surface free of any joins. Cork usually comes in pre-cut tiles, available in a natural finish or a choice of colours, which can be laid in patterns and border motifs. Acrylic tiles, finished in a hard-wearing polyurethane coating, are also popular and can also be laser cut into intricate patterns and designs.

Composites, laminates and glass

Composite materials can sometimes be used on floors, but laminates are far too brittle for this type of heavy-duty use. Glass can be incorporated into flooring schemes, but it is usually only in a small area where an architectural feature has been created to bring light in from a lower level. In cases such as this, thick glass bricks may be set into an area of floor to allow the light to pass through.

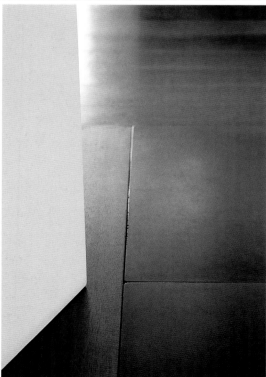

Above left: When you put down floor covering it is a good idea to lay it first, before installing any fitted cabinets. The flooring will run continuously under the units, rather than butting up, perhaps irregularly or unevenly, to the plinth or base of the unit.

Left: Stone tiles have been used in the working part of the kitchen, but in the open plan living area beyond the floor is dressed with rich wooden boards. The stone floor has a wooden edge strip, which helps to make it appear an integral part of overall flooring scheme.

Wood

If possible, wooden floors should be professionally laid on a good smooth, level foundation. Wood floors are warm to walk on, easy to brush and clean and will last for many years. They may also be laid in patterns ranging from lines of straight planks to herringbone, squares, diagonal and brick-style designs. There is also a natural variety of colour, from pale ash, maple and birch to mid-tone oak and dark merabu and mahogany, or the almost black wenge – which is usually used for decorative insets rather than a whole floor. There are also different types of wood flooring. Solid, which is the more expensive, is timber throughout, whereas what is called 'engineered flooring' will have a top layer of hardwood mounted on a base of less expensive soft or plywood. Different finishes for wooden floors include lacquer, usually acrylic or varnish, which gives a high gloss that can be wiped with a damp mop. An oiled floor has oil impregnated into the top layer, and an oiled and waxed finish is an oiled floor with a wax finish added for extra protection. The effect is a softer, more natural appearance than lacquer or varnish.

Metal

Metal flooring has gained in popularity in recent years and usually has a textured, patterned surface to give a better grip underfoot. Steel floors have an industrial feel and rarely sit comfortably in traditional, domestic kitchens.

Left: In open-plan rooms rugs can be used to define different spaces, to create rooms within rooms. Here one mat defines the sitting area while another, lighter-toned one delineates the dining zone.

Above right: Very narrow planks of wooden flooring, laid so that their lines run across a room, can give the impression of added width to a narrow space. If they are laid longways, they can exaggerate the length.

Right: Broad floorboards are best in a larger room; in a small one they can make it appear more cramped and crowded than it is.

NUTS AND BOLTS

Below: Metal surfaces are practical as they are easy to clean, but sharp objects will scratch the surface.

Below right: Zinc was popular in Victorian times and has seen something of a revival. Traditionally, a sheet of zinc was wrapped around a wooden form and secured with tacks or nails.

Right and far right: A marble worktop is cold, easy to wipe clean and will withstand thorough sterilization with boiling water. This makes it an ideal surface on which to make pastry or prepare fish or meat. Also, acid from citrus fruits or red wine will not damage the surface, making it an ideal worktop for a keen cook.

WORKTOPS

The qualities needed in a good worktop surface are ease of cleaning and suitability for contact with hot pans and sharp knives. You need not be restricted to a single material – a mix of surfaces, such as marble and wood insets in a laminate, is often more practical. To help extend the longevity of worktops, always use chopping boards; they protect vulnerable finishes, are a handy size for transporting ingredients to a pot, and can be carried to a sink to be thoroughly scrubbed (see Utensils and Gadgets pages 154–55).

Rock and stone surfaces

Granite is an extremely hard-wearing, heat-resistant washable material with a classic appearance. It is available in a number of finishes, from high gloss to honed, which has a matt look. Marble is more porous than granite so needs to be well finished and sealed; it is also expensive so might be used in conjunction with or as part of a work surface made of another material, such as wood. Slate is a softer material, with varying surface pattern. Slate with high silica content

Top left: A raised wooden stand in the centre of a grey stone worktop is a display area for decorative objects.

Top: When using natural materials such as wood or stone make sure that they all come from one batch, as colour, texture and grain can vary from tree to tree and from one site within a quarry to another.

Left and above: Edges or lips with a smooth rounded finish will make it easier to work close to the worktop.

109

Below right and centre: Highly patterned stone can dominate a scheme, so it is a good idea to contrast it with a plainer surface, such as wood, and to keep the design of the units simple.

Below: With a patterned splashback, single-coloured work surfaces contrast well.

Bottom: Formica comes in many brilliant colours and printed patterns. This man-made material is very tough and heat-resistant, because it is formed from laminated sheets of melamine.

is the most suitable for worktop use and it should be finished and sealed to make sure water and other moisture does not penetrate the surface. Volcanic stone also has natural striations and markings and, as its volcanic origins would suggest, is strong and heat resistant. Recent innovations include the addition of enamel surface glazes, which are also hard wearing and have an attractive and colourful finish, but they are expensive so this inevitably restricts their use. Concrete is heat-resistant and incredibly resilient and it can be poured on site to create some unusual and atypical shapes. Concrete has a porous surface so it must be sealed prior to use to protect it from stains, and it may also be coloured with pigments when it is

mixed to give it a softer, less utilitarian appearance. Concrete should be a minimum depth of 50 mm (2in) to be sturdy enough for a kitchen worktop.

Manmade materials

Composite worktops can be joined by heat-moulding processes so the seam is almost invisible; this also makes it easy to form a continuous surface, introduce curves or form unusual shapes. Integral features such as sinks and drainers can also be moulded into a worktop, so eliminating the usual joints and ridges that require careful cleaning. Laminates are materials formed by being heated, so they have an in-built heat resistance of around 170°C (340°F), but they should

be protected from sharp blades as the surface may mark. Any areas where a section of the laminate has been cut out, for example at a join between two runs of work surface or around a sink, should be carefully sealed to prevent moisture seeping to the backboard, which will swell when wet. When buying laminate to be fitted on a worktop, make sure that the outer edge, the side that will face you, is finished, preferably with a smooth-curved edge, rather than a raw one. Most retailers will also supply a stick-on strip of matching laminate with which to finish side edges. Avoid ribbed or textured laminates, which can be difficult to clean.

Glass
See Wall coverings (pages 101—102).

Wood
This warm, natural product suits both modern and traditional settings well. Wood has natural acidity that inhibits bacterial growth, so it is an ideal surface for a food-preparation area. Wood is easy to cut into any shape and is hard wearing. It also mellows with age and small surface marks generally add to its patina. Hardwoods such as oak, maple, beech and iroko are better for kitchen use than the softer woods, which might warp and bend in very hot steamy conditions. Wooden counters should either be impregnated with sealant or regularly oiled. New surfaces might need regular weekly oiling for the first few months and then an annual or twice-yearly treatment to maintain their condition. All wood in kitchens should be specially dried and cured so that it does not absorb water, as the process of wetting and drying will cause cracking and might also make a wood inset buckle.

Metals
The joins in stainless steel and aluminium worktops are generally welded and therefore watertight, but you will need to use a cutting board to protect the work-tops from scratches. Steel and aluminium surfaces can be sterilized with boiling water, making them an especially hygienic surface on which to prepare food.

Right: This unusual green table top is made from a volcanic rock base with a special fired ceramic finish called Pyrolave, which is extremely heat resistant, hardwearing and available in a wide range of colours.

Below: Recent advances in glass manufacture mean not only can larger sheets of glass be made, avoiding the need for unsightly joins, but also finishing techniques ensure that it is stronger, tougher and safer, therefore ideal for a contemporary kitchen work surface.

CABINETS AND STORAGE

Kitchen storage tends to focus on units that can be wall mounted or floor standing, the latter often also providing the base for the worktop. Most unit bases, also known as carcasses, are mass produced with a chipboard or MDF interior; it is the fronts or doors that give them their style and appearance. The doors can vary from solid wood to laminates (see page 103) and mass-produced units are made in standard sizes.

The better manufacturers supply floor-standing units with adjustable legs so that they can be raised or lowered to a height that is comfortable to work at.

These adjustable legs were frequently disguised by a base plinth, but this is no longer the norm and they are often left exposed as part of a freer, less-fitted look. If you do opt for a plinth, then recess it by about 75mm (3in) so that your feet can slip a little way under the front of the unit. This will make it easier to reach the back section of the work surface on a lower unit, especially for small- to average-height people.

For comfortable access to food preparation areas the upper units should be mounted above head level so that you don't knock your head against them when working. You may also opt to have narrower units or shelves at this level so that they only over-hang the rear part of the working area. As most carcasses come in standard sizes, and rooms don't measure up to match, you may need to add extra elements such as wine racks (see pages 122–23), spice drawers, or even pieces of freestanding furniture.

ALLOCATION OF SPACE

Storage is a major part of the kitchen furniture and can be divided into three different areas. The first is for food: fresh, chilled, frozen, dried and tinned. Next is the equipment involved in food preparation, including utensils – some of these can be kept in drawers, but other frequently used items should be kept on hand. The third is pots and pans, which can be stored in drawers, from hanging rails or kept on open shelves. If they are put on show they must be attractive and contribute to the look of the room rather than detract.

Although storage should be practical it can also be a decorative element, for example in a traditional

Far left: Cupboards are an intrinsic part of the overall appearance of the kitchen. This barrel-shaped one is reminiscent of an Art Deco cocktail cabinet. The inlay and handles marry with other cabinets in the room, though it stands as a piece of freestanding furniture

Below left: A drawer like this is an ideal place to store keys and batteries – small items won't be difficult to find in its limited space.

Below centre: Certain electrical equipment, such as microwaves, can be put in a cupboard, but there must be a good fan system or adequate ventilation to vent away the heat.

Below: In difficult spaces unusual shapes can provide unexpected solutions. Here gently curved doors follow the line of the double sink.

Right: Storage should be divided into a number of compartments, based on different use. For example, small drawers should be allocated for holding knives and forks and roll-top units are ideal for items such as toasters and coffee-makers so that they can be pulled forward when needed, but pushed back behind the doors when not in use.

NUTS AND BOLTS

Below: Long rail handles run across the full width of these drawers, so they can be opened from any point.

Below centre: Waste bins for wet and dry stuff will make recycling easier. Tins, bottles and plastic can go in one bin and be disposed of as appropriate, while wet waste is kept separate.

Bottom and below right: Deep drawers with strong supportive brackets can contain cooking pots, sieves and casseroles under the hob, whereas lighter, more shallow ones are useful for keeping mugs, glasses or sets of cups and saucers.

or rustic-style kitchen shelves and racks may be used to house, but also display, attractive china and glass. Even in the most contemporary surroundings, a row of matching containers for coffee, tea and sugar or a line of sparkling glass tumblers or simple white bowls will break up the uniformity of cool steel surfaces.

The best way to organize kitchen storage is to allocate specific areas to items related to the task or tasks that take place there. For example, the sink and the dishwasher should be close together as they will probably use the same or parallel water supplies and waste outlets. At this point you should have an under-sink cupboard for detergents and washing-related products. Close to the dishwasher is also the most appropriate place to store your plates, china, glass-ware and cutlery, because on a daily basis you will

need to take these items from the machine when they are clean and store them until they are next required. The sink area is also where fruit and vegetables are washed and peeled and scraps or leftovers scraped off plates before they are slotted into the dishwasher, and because of these activities it is also useful to have the waste bin situated here.

FOOD STORAGE

Food storage may be fragmented. Dried and tinned goods can be kept in a cool area in almost any part of the room, whereas chilled and frozen foods must be kept in a refrigerator or freezer. Ideally, both the refrigerator and the freezer should be positioned away from the cooker and hob because of the heat which might adversely affect the chilling mechanisms.

Fresh foods can also be stored in the chill drawer of the refrigerator, but other items such as onions and certain vegetables are best kept in the open in a cool, dark and dry location such as a wire rack shelf within a cupboard or a covered wicker basket. This type of container allows air to circulate around the contents, which helps to prevent mould from occurring.

The refrigerator and fresh food storage are best kept near the area of work surface where most food preparation will take place, and if possible close to the sink so that the food itself, hands and preparation boards can be easily washed. If there is additional space available elsewhere within the kitchen, or in an adjacent passage way or utility room, you might choose to have a second larger fridge-freezer there, in which to store long-term produce such as frozen meat and vegetables, pastry, water, soft drinks, beer and wine. Have a smaller, under-unit refrigerator in the food preparation area for more frequently used items, such as milk and butter.

Also near this crucial area of food preparation. it is appropriate to have a drawer for utensils, such as a vegetable peeler, apple corer and items needed when getting meals ready or baking. A couple of chopping boards and a knife rack or block containing a range of sharp kitchen knives will be essential.

Left: The upper section of this built-in dresser has deep shelves ideal for larger items of tableware or dried and tinned goods. The first row of drawers is small and could be used for cutlery, while the deeper ones are ideal for linens. Try to store items in the right size space.

Above: A neat column of drawers is useful for storing cutlery and drying cloths.

Below: Try to measure the amount of storage you will actually need rather than build it first and then fill it. Possessions always expand to fill available space.

Above: These full-height cabinets hold impressive amounts of tableware

Above centre: Glass doors can appear less dense and heavy and are useful in a small kitchen, but items stored behind even opaque glass must be well arranged.

Above right: Here a mix of solid and glass-fronted cupboards provide storage for the attractive as well as more mundane items. The configuration of base and wall units alludes to the traditional dresser shape.

Pots, pans and utensils used when cooking should be stored as close as possible to the oven, hob and hot plates. Pots and pans tend to be bulky and on the whole not a great asset to the overall appearance of a kitchen, so are best stored out of sight. In many modern kitchens there are deep drawers under the hob, lined with removable rubber mats that can be taken out and washed. These deep drawers mean that even the largest casserole can be contained yet be close at hand when needed.

DOORS AND SHELVES
Doors are a practical way of concealing the contents of a cupboard and protecting them from moisture and

grease that accumulates with time, but they are also a major decorative element and have a significant impact on the overall appearance of the room.

Doors can be made of wood, or faced with steel or one of the many laminates and veneers you can choose from, but too many solid-fronted doors and wall-mounted units will make a room seem dark and oppressive, especially a small room. By using glass panel insets in the centre of some of the doors, and mixing cupboards with open shelving, you can create a lighter and brighter look. But it is not advisable to use glass doors on lower-level units, where they may be subjected to bangs and kicks. In a small kitchen, consider sliding or roll-top cupboard doors as these

will not encroach on valuable floor space. Even fabric can be a useful replacement for the doors on floor cabinets, as it is soft and will allow anyone preparing food on the worktop closer access.

Shelves can be made of many materials – such as glass, steel, concrete or wood – but they should never be positioned directly over hobs or grills as you might burn your arm stretching over a flame or hot surface to retrieve something from the shelf. This location is also prone to grease and condensation, which will quickly make an open shelf grimy. Glass shelves are useful in small kitchens because they look light and airy, but they should only be made from reinforced or laminated glass if they are to have the strength and resilience for this working location.

Above and above left: This flat wall of storage divides into many separate cupboards with doors that hinge either out or upward. The lightweight doors have been faced with laminated textured fabric that allows the ceiling lights to shine through and illuminate the contents of the cupboard.

Far left and left: An area that is often neglected is the potentially wasted space beneath the stairs. Here it has been used to provide an expanse of storage as well as a separate cloakroom.

117

NUTS AND BOLTS

HANDLES

Handles are a small but important element in the overall scheme of a kitchen and they offer an opportunity to stamp your individual style on a uniform cupboard. A plain unit door can be decorated with an unusual handle that will make the overall appearance much more interesting and, conversely, a colourful or ornate door may be toned down by a simple, elegantly designed fitting

But above all decorative and styling requirements, handles must first and foremost be easy to grasp and simple to clean. Handles should also be rounded rather than sharp and angular because from time to time you will inevitably bump up against one or open a door too forcefully and hit yourself. This is also a considerable factor in kitchens where small children may have access.

The most commonly used material in contemporary kitchens is stainless steel, but cupboard handles can also be made in brass, iron, chrome, ceramic and resin. Resin offers an almost limitless range of colours and shapes, from round and tear drop ones to star shaped. Resin is warm and relatively soft to the touch, and its appearance can be an asset in a plainly decorated room. Even metal handles have come a long way from the standard, plain bar and knob. There are jokey designs such as those featuring knife, fork and spoon shapes, cross-bar styles and textured finishes.

Below left: These recessed steel circular handles, reminiscent of portholes, were chosen to endorse a nautical theme in the room's décor.

Below right: You can mix and match handles on the same row of cabinets, using long tubular handles on tall doors and disc handles on smaller cupboards.

Right: Plexiglass and other glass-like, man-made materials can be molded and formed into interesting and unusual handle shapes. These opaque resin handles appear to glow in artificial light and take on a luminescent quality.

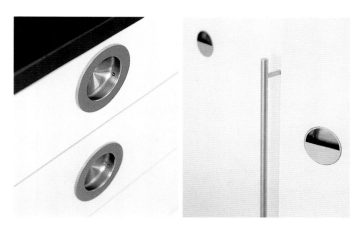

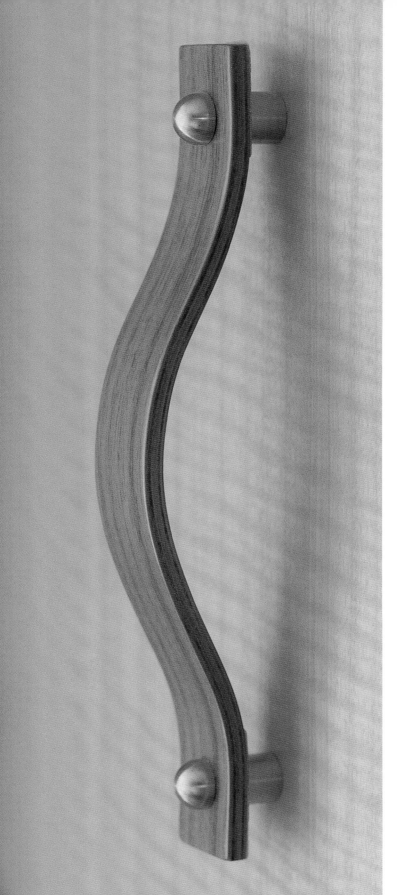

If you are tempted to go for a fun or unusual element in your kitchen, or add a personalized touch, such as your initials, or a teapot design to complement a collection, then the handles are probably the best feature to play with. They can be inexpensive and are also easy to change when the novelty wears off or when you come to sell your home and need a less idiosyncratic appearance to the kitchen.

If you are going for a more classic option, the most practical designs are the simplest; the classic 'D' handle does everything required of it and can be found in polished or matt metal finishes as well as composite, resin and wood. Knobs or rounded shapes are also inoffensive and in wood are part of the rustic or traditional style, but they might be difficult to grasp when hands are wet or greasy.

Some cupboard doors do not have handles at all; instead they have a small recess at the top or bottom of the door that can be used to grip and pull. Or they may have a spring-catch mechanism that is operated simply by pressing on the door to make it open. There are also designs that incorporate a slim-line lip in the end of the metal trim along the edge of the door, the lip section providing just enough height and depth for fingers to grasp. These options make it easy to clean the door, but also leave the surface plain and unadorned, an effect most often utilized in minimalist kitchens where clean, uninterrupted planes are paramount.

Left: This pleasingly curved, almost sculptural, wooden door handle, with its visible grain, is testament to the inherent beauty of wood.

Below left: This traditional style of handle remains popular because it does the job it was designed for and doesn't catch on fabric or anything that sweeps past it. It adds a suitably low-key finish to classically styled drawers.

Below right: A small decorative drawer knob, such as this organically shaped metal one, is most suited to a linen or cutlery drawer.

NUTS AND BOLTS

Below: An open plate rack is appropriate in this style of kitchen and it is ideal in a busy family home where plates and dishes are almost constantly in use and need to be readily accessible.

Right and far right: The low beamed ceiling in this farmhouse-style kitchen has been utilized to create an unusual rack to hold wine glasses. Short lengths of wood have been attached to the beam, and the foot of each glass simply slots in between the struts.

SAFETY AND ERGONOMICS

A few important warnings to take into consideration when planning and locating storage are as follows: Firstly, keep chemicals, sharp and heavy objects out of the reach of children. There are a number of good childproof door catches that can easily be fitted to floor-level cupboards that prevent them from being easily accessible; otherwise place these items in wall-mounted cupboards, well above their height.

Secondly, if you are contemplating wall-mounted units above the worktop make sure that you allow enough head height for the tallest member of your household to be comfortable working there – even if it is only to make a cup of tea. Thirdly, do not place all your cast-iron casseroles in the same wall-mounted cupboard, as the combined weight might cause the shelves, and even the cupboard itself, to become

dislodged. Try to distribute weight evenly among various cupboards and drawers. Fourthly, do not fix wall units directly above hobs: the heat and steam will damage the base of the unit and cause rising vapour to skirt around the cupboard and into your face.

Another important factor to consider when you are locating units is to make sure that their doors do not open on top of each other or hinder access to any other appliance. For example, test that you can open the dishwasher door, which generally comes down, while still being able to open the cupboard doors on either side so that you can put things directly from the machine onto their storage shelf. Another area that can be problematic is a unit placed close to main access doors: avoid these being positioned so that when someone comes into the kitchen, the door catches or slams a cupboard door behind it.

The fine tuning of storage also involves placing plugs and sockets close to areas where they will be used. For example, if you have a toaster, kettle and coffee-maker you will need sockets beside the place where they are used. You will also require sockets for machines such as the dishwasher and refrigerator or

Top: In a kitchen such as this, where there are few doors on the cupboards, it is essential to have adequate extraction or venting to remove steam and moisture that might cause dishes and plates on open shelves to become grimy. Crockery should be stored well away from the hob and oven to avoid grease settling.

Above left: A metal stand supports glass shelves on which oils and spices used in cooking are kept readily to hand. The glass is easy to wipe clean if the oil drips or if the spices are spilt.

Above: Storage can slot into all sorts of niches; for example, these shelves and grid recesses have been built around a chimney and disused fireplace.

Above: Even a corridor can house extra storage. For example, on either side of this passageway leading to a small dining area are rows of painted shelves stacked with matching Kilner jars, plain white china and wine glasses. The symmetry and discipline create interest and the shelves are an asset.

freezer, but don't position electrical sockets too close to sinks or hobs where water or high temperatures may damage the wiring to the sockets.

WINE RACKS

There are many types of wine rack – wall-mounted, internal and floor standing – in a range of materials, usually selected to suit the style of the décor and the space available. Wall-mounted racks do not use up valuable counter space and some versions can also be used to store bottled oils, vinegars and mineral water. Lightweight chrome and steel racks come in many guises. There are the solid panel styles with small holes into which the necks of the bottles are placed, there are also wire designs with oval supports onto which the bottles are laid, and other designs that hold the bottle horizontally between and neck and base support. These minimal metal wine racks suit most styles of décor because they are simple and understated, but they are perhaps most appropriate to the low-key and modern kitchens.

Although wall-mounted racks are economical on space, you can also use an area of wine storage to fill in the gaps that are left between, or at the end of a run of, standard-size units. Most shell or carcass cupboards come in standard sizes and may not fit exactly along the full length of a wall. This unfilled and potentially dead area could be the perfect place in which to locate a purpose-built wine rack .

Below: This custom-made cabinet acts as a partial room divider, but it is also a bottle and glass store, and when there is a party in the apartment it becomes a bar.

Below right: The upper corner of this kitchen has been fitted with a tailor-made wine rack that holds up to three dozen bottles, so freeing up a lot of lower-level storage. The back of the compartmented unit has been sectioned off at bottle length so that the bottles don't disappear into the full depth of the recess, because it would otherwise reach all the way back into the corner of the room.

Wine racks can be tall and narrow, a single or two-bottle width, or long and wide so they fit in between a worktop and lower drawer. Most of these space-filling bottle holders are tailor-made and constructed in wood or MDF and then painted, stained or finished to complement the trim or facing of the units.

You can buy, as part of a fully-fitted kitchen, wine trays with a pull-out mechanism that allows the wines to be easily selected. These are popular because they are shallow, only a few centimetres deeper than the wine bottle, and are therefore space effective.

Terracotta or brick racks are usually stacked up at floor level. These bottle holders are cylindrical on the inside and octagonal on the outside and can be stacked up in a square, oblong or pyramid shape. If individual holders are soaked in cold water they will chill the wine bottle stored inside.

Another option is an old-fashioned wooden beer or bottle crate. These hold up to a dozen bottles and usually have small recesses at the side to make them easier to pick up and carry. The wooden crate was originally designed to sit on its base, but it can be set on its side, which is the preferred way to store wine – it enables the wine to keep the cork moist and expanded, which creates a good seal in the neck of the bottle. Thise type of bottle holder is compatible with the rustic or farmhouse style of kitchen.

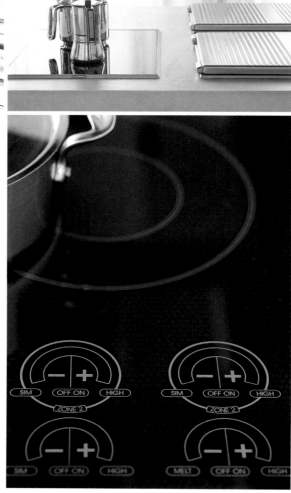

Above: Control dials can be positioned either on the top of the hob in a panel to one side of the rings, or on a front panel. You are more likely to bump into them on the front and possibly turn on or increase the heat by accident, but the advantage is the dials are less likely to become greasy.

Above right: Griddles and hotplates can be sunk into a counter top and may have a lid or covering that protects them when not in use.

Right: Ceramic hobs have a smooth easy-wipe surface, but should only be cleaned with a recommended cream that is abrasive free.

COOKERS, FANS AND FRIDGES

The type of cooker you choose will be governed by the sort of cooking you enjoy, the type of fuel available to you and the size of your kitchen. Although you can get bottled gas, homes that are not on a direct gas supply might, for ease, opt for a solely electrically operated cooking system. But many people, and especially keen cooks, prefer the visual contact of the gas flame, which enables them to judge the level of heat and to alter it immediately. To cater for those who like the ease and control of gas for hob cooking and grilling, but enjoy the regular and even temperature

available with electricity for the oven, there are an increasing number of dual-fuel range cookers that offer a combination of the two types of power source.

The appearance of the cooker is also important, especially if you consider it is the single largest piece of equipment that is usually the focus of the room. By the time you have assembled the cooker, extractor fan and hood, a splashback and perhaps a rail with a line of shining stainless-steel accessories, it is little wonder that is the point to which the eye is drawn.

The style and finish of the cooker will also need to blend in with the rest of your scheme. If you choose a country or rustic style kitchen, you might opt for a traditional enamelled range, whereas in the currently

Left: Steam cookery is becoming an increasingly popular cooking method, especially with those people interested in healthy living and Oriental-style dishes.

Below: This traditional combined cooker and hob fits neatly into the available space in this small kitchen.

popular cook's kitchen there is more likely to be an industrial or commercial-style range with a stainless-teel or brushed aluminium façade. But size might also be a deciding factor, in which case conventional and wall-mounted cookers should be considered.

CONVENTIONAL OVEN

This style is free-standing and generally around 60cm (24in) wide and 90cm (36in) high. The oven can be powered by electric or gas, and can be fan assisted. Fan-assisted or Circotherm cooking uses a fan at the back of the oven to circulate the hot air inside and give a regular, overall temperature (hot air rises so in non-fan ovens the bottom of the oven may be cooler than the top). There is usually a glass panel in the door so you can view the contents without opening the door and lowering the temperature, and a light.

Above the oven is a hob with three or four rings; these can be electrical plates or gas burners. There may be an eye-level grill or a grill function in the oven. Many conventional ovens have a lid that closes over the hob when it is not in use, keeping the surface of the hob clean and providing an additional worktop area. This type of cooker is good for a small flat or a first-time buyer's home – it has all the basic functions required to cook but is compact and self contained.

WALL-MOUNTED OVENS

Wall-mounted or built-in ovens allow the various different functions of the conventional cooker to be split up into descrete elements, which can then be located in separate parts of the room. The oven might be fixed into a wall unit at eye-level height; this can make it easier to work with than the low-level version,

Above left: This cooker has been designed to have a professional appearance, but is adapted for domestic use; it has the overall looks and style of a commercial cooker on a reduced scale.

Left: These very powerful stoves should always be used in conjunction with an appropriately sized exhaust hood and ventilator, which will remove cooking smells and excess steam.

Right: As an alternative to a single large stove, lack of space or your personal style of cooking might dictate that two smaller ovens are preferable. Here a pair of wall-mounted ovens are set one above the other and a microwave, set into a unit over the hob, provides yet another option.

Below and right: Facilities for three different direct-heat cooking methods are incorporated into this free-standing work unit – there is a single gas burner, a flat hot plate and a griddle. The oven and microwave built into the wall units further increase the flexibility and scope of cooking options.

because you can check on food and put dishes into the oven and take them out without bending down. Wall-mounted ovens can be single (average size around 558mm [22½in] wide, 545mm [21½in] deep and 567mm [22¾in] high) or double (890mm [36in] high, 595mm [24in] wide and 560mm [22½in] deep). The recess or carcass in which they are set will need an electrical socket and extractor ducting. They might also incorporate many other alternatives, such as a grill, rotisserie and a self-cleaning function.

Steam cooking is another option. This is a relatively new facility, but one that is fast growing in popularity because it offers a healthy approach to cooking as it requires little or no fat to undertake. The food is cooked in 80 per cent humidity, so it retains moisture, and it is almost impossible to burn food cooked in this way.

HOBS

In conjunction with the wall-mounted oven there is a hob; this is generally installed in a section of worktop, operated by gas or electricity. Gas hobs have four to six burners set into a metal or enamel plate with raised pan supports. They come in 60, 70 and 90cm (24, 28 and 36in) sizes and require a depth of between 2 and 4 cm (¾ and 1¾in) to allow them to be recessed into the worktop. Electric hobs traditionally have solid metal plates or coils that heat up, but ceramic hobs have become more common place. The ceramic hob is a single surface under which the electric rings are located. The advantage of this set up is that you can quickly and simply wipe the surface clean, but specific ceramic cleaners are advised as the surface may be easily scratched and damaged.

RANGES

Traditional cast-iron ranges with enamelled panels can be run off natural or bottled gas, oil, electricity or solid fuel. Well insulated, they retain heat efficiently, creating a radiant heat that is less severe to cook with than direct-fuel flame or electrical element sources.

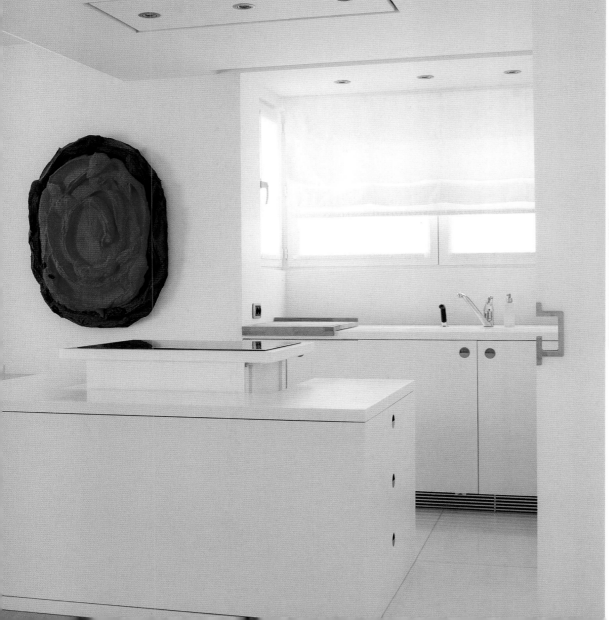

Left and above: This hob and cooker are controlled by a hydraulically operated system so they can be raised or lowered. The cooking station can be adjusted to a comfortable height for who-ever works in the kitchen at the push of a button. When not in use, the hob slides down to fit snugly into the work surface and become an integral part of the unit.

129

Below and below centre: Fridges and freezers come in many sizes, but the large American-style refrigerators are increasingly popular. They take up floor space, but free up shelf storage because they hold so much.

Centre: Steel is most often the preferred finish, but you could make a decorative feature of your fridge by covering it with a pattern, such as these map pages.

Below right: An external ice and cold water dispenser makes these staples easily accessible so the door does not have to be constantly opened, which will lower the temperature inside.

But they are heavy, and if installed in an upper-floor apartment they might require extra structural support. This type of range can also provide central heating and hot water, but might be too hot as a heat source and cooking facility in a small kitchen in the summer.

The standard range or semi-professional cooker runs off gas, electricity or a combination of the two. Modern configurations include six ring burners and specialist facilities for wok cooking and fish kettles. The new ranges are less heavy than cast-iron ones and have stainless-steel or aluminium façades.

REFRIGERATORS AND FREEZERS

The standard combination fridge-freezer is a narrow unit approximately 1779mm (6ft) high, 550mm (22in) deep and 540mm (21½in) wide. On one level is the fridge with a capacity of around 211 litres (46 gallons).

Inside the fridge door there are usually small fixed shelves whereas in the main body the shelves are adjustable. Many styles also have two drawers at the bottom where food that needs to be cool but not fully chilled can be kept. The other half of the unit contains a separate freezer compartment with a capacity of around 82 litres (18 gallons).

From the standard single-unit fridge-freezer there are a number of variations where the two elements have been separated or re-structured. For example, the functions may be split and arranged side by side in two smaller units under a section of work surface. You can also find single tall fridge units, of fridge-freezer size, and similarly sized units that are solely freezers, which can provide ample capacity for the requirements of a large family. The arrangement and volume will depend on the size of your family, the

amount of fresh food you buy versus frozen foods, how often you shop and the space available.

American refrigerators tend to be much larger – generally double the width of the standard European fridge-freezer – and double as a larder facility, being used to store opened jars and packet goods as well as to keep raw and fresh produce cool. Where there isn't space to accommodate a single unit of this capacity, the different refrigeration functions can be subdivided into a number of smaller machines. For example, there may be a drinks cooler for beers, wine and soft drinks, another chill unit for fruit, vegetables, cheeses and diary products that would be damaged by too intense cold, and then cool accommodation for jars, packets and other foodstuffs.

Although they are often large, not all these units need to be concealed; indeed, many are attractive and they can be an asset to the overall look of your kitchen, or even the focal point. A wide range of fridges and freezers are now available with colourful facings, some even designed in retro 1950s style. Stainless steel, silver, red, green and even pink are all on offer. But, if you prefer a uniform appearance to the room, you can set the unit inside a carcass and attach a panel to match the rest of the units.

FANS AND VENTS

With hobs and range-style cookers you will need to install a way of removing the steam and smell from the kitchen; the most effective way is an extractor fan placed directly above the heat source. There are two main types of extractor fan: one recycles air through a charcoal filter and the other, more efficient, option, removes smoke and steam through a vent ducted to the outside, taking away food smells and moisture.

A good extractor fan will expel around 500m³ of air per hour when placed over a standard cooker or hob. Range cookers and semi-professional styles will need a correspondingly larger extractor, something than can cope with around 1100–1200m³ per hour, otherwise the kitchen with become smoky every time you cook and unpleasant smells will linger.

Above: This large central working unit incorporates a wide ceramic hob – this surface style of cookery can create a lot of steam and heat so it is important to have an effective extractor fan. Otherwise the kitchen will become damp and unpleasantly hot to work in. Many types of extractor fans have filter panels of absorbent material which will soak up the air-borne grease; these filters must be changed regularly.

Below: A decorative glass splashback with an etched striped design contains any splashes and spray that are generated in this curved double sink unit.

Below right: Gauge the size of sink you will need according to the tasks to be performed. This copper sink is in a bar area, and it is used primarily for rinsing.

PLUMBING

The kitchen is an area where three potentially lethal elements – water, electricity and fire – come together, so it is important that all plumbing and wiring is undertaken by professionals with accredited qualifications and good references. All newly purchased machines should come with guarantees that cover at least the initial period of use, and these may be extended. To ensure the validity of these guarantees, and the good working of your machine, you should read and follow the manufacturer's instructions fully. Don't assume because you used your old washing machine in one way the same programmes apply to the new version.

SINKS

The wet work of a kitchen should be focused around one area, where there is access to an outside wall for cold water supply and waste outlets. The sink is the most visible sign of this section and is often placed by a window, firstly because this ensures an exterior wall, but also because in the days before dishwashers the person working at the sink had something to look out on as well as access to daylight.

The decisions to make about the type of sink you select are concerned mainly with size and material. If you have a dishwasher you may only need a single sink with a draining board on one side. But if you have a large family and cook frequently, using many pots and pans, a double sink with central waste-disposal unit and a drainer either side might be necessary to supplement the capacity of the dishwasher.

Dishwashers are good for the bulk of everyday cutlery, china and glassware, but lead crystal, bone handle cutlery and heavy pots are not really suitable

for machine washing. Cast-iron pots, which can be adversely affected by the very high salt content and chemicals in detergents, and heavily stained dishes which need pre-soaking, are best tackled in the sink.

Once you have calibrated the size of sink you need, look at the styles and types of material on offer. Sinks can be pre-formed from stainless steel with integral drainers, but will need to be set into a work surface and sealed with a flexible filler. Steel sinks come in a variety of shapes, including round and oblong, and they can be formed in draining panels that slot into awkward spaces such as corners.

Ceramic kitchen sinks are not that common, but are still used in the deep and oblong style known as the Belfast sink, which is appropriate in traditional kitchen schemes. There are also composite sinks, many made as part of a run of work surface and with integral drainer surfaces, smoothly formed without a join so there are no problems with cleaning.

TAPS AND SPOUTS

Taps for a kitchen sink should be as simple and as functional as possible, and they should be suitably positioned so that the spout or spouts are well above the sink so that you do not crack or break glass and

Top left: This circular sink has a removable chopping board lid. Waste vegetable matter can be swept off the board and into the sink, where it is macerated by the waste-disposal system.

Above: These deep double sinks are set into an island unit that is also an informal dining area. The deep sinks mean that a certain amount of washing up can be left in the base, where it won't be easily visible.

Right: A single wooden worktop runs around a sink and waste unit, making it easier to wipe down and clean. Wood is good surface near a sink area because it is soft in comparison to stone and marble, so might prevent cracks and chips in china and glass, but any wood that comes in regular contact with water should be well sealed and finished.

Right: Corners are often difficult areas to use, but here a sink has been sited to run diagonally across one. The sink is set into a work surface of durable water-resistant marble.

Below right: There are various accessories you can use in conjunction with a sink; this metal colander is designed to rest on the rim of the sink, directly under the water flow from the single-spout tap. Freshly washed foodstuffs can then be left to drain.

Below: With separate sinks that are set below the work surface, rather than part of it, it is important that the join between them is water-tight and secure.

Above: Double sinks allow soiled pots and pans to soak in one side, while the other can be used for filling the kettle or rinsing vegetables. These sinks also each have individual taps rather then the usual shared spout that will swivel over two sinks, so that they can both be used at any one time.

Right: The flow of water from this single-lever tap is controlled by up and down movement, and temperature by a sideways adjustment.

Far right: Taps should be easy to operate, especially if you have greasy or wet hands. Traditional-style, ceramic-handled levers can be pushed on and off using the forearm or back of a hand when necessary.

china against them when placing them in the bowl. In many modern kitchens there is often the additional feature of a nozzle attachment on a flexible hose, which sprays water directly into the base of a pot or pan or over vegetables being cleaned.

Wall-mounted taps and a movable spout offer a very safe combination, but check that the taps are not positioned too high, otherwise the force of the water hitting the sink will cause it to splash. Taps can also be plumbed to one side or in the corner of the worktop surround into which the sink is set. This arrangement ensures that they are not immediately in the line of access to the bowl.

The other thing to consider with taps is that your hands may be greasy or covered with flour when you come to use them, so a very simple push or lever mechanism is preferable to a smoothly rounded knob, which could be difficult to grasp and turn. Also consider ease of cleaning: the more decorative and complex the tap head the more difficult it will be to tackle thoroughly. The single swan-neck-style spout with one shared lever tap that moves from right to left to switch the water temperature from hot to cold will minimize the amount of hardware for cleaning.

WASTE-DISPOSAL UNITS

Waste-disposal units are usually situated directly beside, or incorporated as part of, the main sink. They are compact machines with macerators which pulp soft residual matter and wash it away through the general waste outlet. They can considerably reduce the amount of waste that you accumulate and in a small flat or upper-storey apartment where you might have to transport rubbish to a central shoot or carry it down several levels to a communal waste outlet, this can be a considerable saving on time and effort.

If you do have a waste-disposal make sure it is regularly used, even if you only wash used dishwater through it every day, otherwise an accumulation of small bits of decomposing waste can remain stuck in the system and cause unpleasant smells.

WASHING MACHINES

Washing machine are sometimes plumbed into kitchens, but most people prefer to have them in a separate laundry or utility room, where the noise of the spin programme cannot interrupt dinner, piles of unsorted laundry can be kept out of sight and freshly washed and ironed clothes will not pick up cooking smells. As well as the pipes for intake and out-flowing water, washing machines with integral tumble-drying programmes will require a separate vent for steam and hot-air emissions – this should preferably be ducted through an external wall.

Below left: A tap raised well above a sink will give good clear access to the sink itself, but if it is set too high running water might splash up and wet anyone who is standing at the sink.

Below: This double sink is served by a mono-block spout and lever tap; the spout can be swung from one sink to the other.

NUTS AND BOLTS

Right: By facing a dish-washer with the same finish as other units in the kitchen it will be less obtrusive.

Below right: If you are limited by space, or your lifestyle is such that you do not need a large-capacity machine, select one of the many slimline dishwashers available. But you must still allow plenty of room for the door to open fully.

Far right: For ease of use site your dishwasher near the sink so waste food can be scraped off and rinsed away before dishes go into the machine. Also place it near to where your china and glassware is stored to simplify unloading.

Rather than rigid copper or metal piping many of these machines are plumbed in with plastic or flexible hoses, which allow for movement when the machine vibrates during spin-drying or tumble-washing cycles. During such movement, which can be considerable in older models, rigid pipes might fracture or break at the joint with the machine, whereas the softer pipes will move easily in any direction. The disadvantage of flexible pipes is that they might unhook or become detached, so it is worth checking the connections are still intact on a regular basis.

DISHWASHERS AND WATER SOFTENERS

Depending on where you live and the type of water you have you may find that a built-in water softener is a good idea. These can be attached to the main cold water inlet and will soften all water before it reaches the taps or machines. Hard water damages heating and other elements by causing a build up of calcium and other minerals, which appears as a hard white crust. It also makes water more scummy, leaving marks around the sink and it has an effect on the quantity used, and results achieved by, detergents.

Dishwashers, available in 12, 8 or 6 place setting sizes with a variety of washing programmes, from light to intensive, will need more or less salt and detergent depending on the hardness of the water supply. Take

advice from the manufacturer's local agent, or the plumber who installs the machine, as to whether a water softener or filter would be advantageous.

HEATING

Heating is another element of plumbing that needs to be carefully planned ahead and installed before any units are put in or flooring and tiles laid. The kitchen is generally well heated, because of the heat emitted by the lighting, oven, hob and other machines in use. In fact, a good ventilation system is often required to reduce heat when the room is fully operational.

Wall space is often at a premium in the kitchen because wall-mounted storage cabinets take priority. Increasingly, people are opting for under-floor heating, especially if the floor surface is hard and cold, such as stone or marble. But if you do not want to take this route, you could look at heat convection units that fit in behind skirting-board size panels and waft warm air at floor level, which then rises and heats the room. Wall-mounted radiators are another possibility, but rather than the traditional flat, horizontal panels, look at ladder-style and vertical radiators which are tall and slender and take up less room.

Below: An island unit is a freestanding cabinet, often placed in the centre of large kitchens to provide a mid point between two sections of worktop.

Right: A mobile unit fitted with lockable wheels can be positioned where needed. It may also double as a trolley when collecting foodstuffs from one side of the room and transporting them to the other,. or to a table.

Below right: This island unit has been designed to be decorative as well as fully functional. It appears like a tall table but it has a sink recessed into its surface and it is also adjacent to the refrigerators and two store cupboards for ease of work.

FREESTANDING FURNITURE

The amount of freestanding furniture found in kitchens increases and declines in an almost cyclical way. In the past, kitchens were made of an assortment of cupboards, tables and shelves, often mis-matched bits and pieces in utilitarian scrubbed pine, providing basic storage and work surfaces. In the 1970s and 1980s the trend was more for fully fitted kitchens with everything bolted to the floor and hung off the wall. Plinths made sure the base of every unit met with the floor and the tops of units reached to the ceiling. The appearance was of uniformity and made-to-measure tailoring that accounted for every inch of space.

More recently the two approaches have merged, with a number of fitted units, usually those containing machines that require a stable foundation for wiring or plumbing, combined with a number of unfitted ones. The advantage with this mix is that you can take some

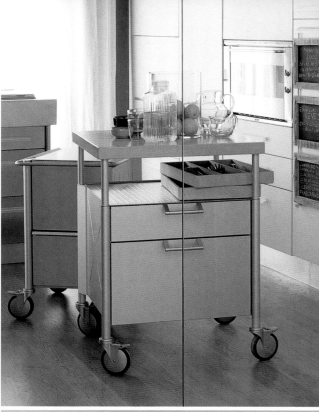

pieces of furniture with you if you move home. Also, if you are working on a limited budget, you can buy key units and add the rest as your finances allow, rather than having to commit to all the fixtures at once.

This open approach to built-in and freestanding furniture also enables you to mix old and new pieces, old for the patina of time and the visual impact, and new pieces for the ease, efficiency and advantages that modern designs offer. Mixing old and new also creates a really personal and individual style.

CUPBOARDS

Among the larger items of freestanding furniture is the classic dresser, with its open shelves on the top for displaying decorative ceramics, a deep surface area beneath and enclosed cupboards with doors at the base. This type of furniture is perennially popular in traditional or country-style kitchens.

Left: Cupboards come in many styles. The white painted one is based on a traditional design; simple and spacious, it is divided into two sections, the upper with glass insets in the door and the bottom with solid panels. It forms a pleasing juxtaposition with the more ornate roll-top style wooden cupboard next to it.

Below: This antique-style French armoire has been converted into a complete mini-kitchen; there is a sink, a microwave, and a small fridge for perishable goods. But when the doors are shut it is simply an elegant piece of furniture.

A small square table can also be helpful in restricted space, but a number of same-sized tables can be used to create a variety of seating configurations. For example, four small square tables can be lined up to form a good-size rectangular or linear format or grouped together into a larger square. You could also create 'L' and 'T' shapes or reduce the size of the oblong table to suit a smaller party, simply by taking one or two of the tables away.

Also space-effective in small rooms is a foldaway table. This is usually semicircular and can be attached to the wall along the straight edge. The rounded edge is then lifted up and supported on a hinged leg that comes out from the wall. When the table is no longer needed the support can be returned to the wall and the table top left to hang down in front.

Above: Buit-in upholstered benches create an inviting dining space and they can fit flexible numbers.

Right: In a more formal dining area, where people will sit and linger over a meal, make sure that the chairs are comfortable, with a cushioned or suspended base and supportive back.

Below right: Although most cooks walk around the kitchen while working, a stool can be a useful perch when peeling vegetables or fruit or for preparing more complex dishes.

Armoires, or large cupboards with solid decoratively panelled doors, are often used in lieu of a pantry to hold dried and tinned goods, or sometimes linen, crockery and glassware. Original antique armoires are usually French in origin, but reproductions with aged, painted exteriors are available. Contemporary freestanding cupboards might have laminate sliding doors or opaque glass insets that match or contrast with the rest of the units in the kitchen.

TABLES

For obvious reasons, tables are perhaps the most ubiquitous piece of unfitted furniture in a kitchen and the shape, size and finish is usually chosen to co-ordinate with the rest of the room. The traditional kitchen table is a long rectangular wooden structure, often with drawers at either end or at one side. This type of table doubles as an extra work surface and can be scrubbed and polished many times.

Round tables are useful in smaller kitchens and can double as a sociable dining table for supper and dinner. When odd numbers of people are dining, a round table counters the problem of a single person being left stranded at the end, and it is said that you can seat more people comfortably at a round table than an oblong one of a similar area.

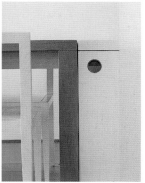

Left and below: This simple and angular style of table and dining chairs is in keeping with this clean white uncluttered room. The generously sized table is on wheels so that is can be pulled into a central position when the ends are needed to bring the seating capacity up to ten. Siting the table near the kitchen means it can also be used as additional work surface.

Far left: Although dining chairs and stools may be stored away neatly under a table, do allow adequate space for them to be pulled out and for people to move around behind them when they are in use.

Left: With tall stools it is important to have a rung or bar at the base of the legs or under the bench or work surface, so that anyone who sits on them has a place to rest their feet.

CHAIRS AND STOOLS

Chairs are necessary to go around any table that is to be used for dining and the chairs are usually chosen to be in keeping with the style of the table, although there are some classic designs, both modern and traditional, that work well with a wide range of tables.

Among the most popular classic chairs is the Arne Jacobsen Series 7 model. It was first produced in 1955, but it still looks as good beside a modern glass and chrome table as it does under a polished wood antique one. Robin Day's Polyprop design is another contemporary favourite, as is the ubiquitous canvas and wood folding style of director's chair. The Bentwood beech seats with woven cane designed by Michael Thonet in 1859, genuinely antique or in contemporary reproduction, are also acceptable with many types of table and they have clean fluid lines that make them a strong contributing element to the overall scheme of the room.

Top: A mobile circular stool can be used to move from one side of the room to another while seated.

Above and above right: These tall stools have well-weighted bases, which will prevent them from toppling over, and curved supportive backrests as part of the seats.

Upper right: Adjustable stools are user friendly as their height can be raised or lowered by turning the seat, which has a long corkscrew-type mechanism.

Lower right: In this very contemporary-style kitchen, wooden blocks provide the seating. They can also be used as occasional tables or a plinth on which to place a decorative object.

What all these classic chairs have in common is their simple shape and style, and that they are lightweight and easy to move. These seats also have a certain amount of 'give' when you sit on them, as well as support, which makes them comfortable to rest on for prolonged periods, such as a meal time. And it is because they fulfil these basic but important criteria that their popularity endures.

There are also many good contemporary chairs using ergonomic design and new materials. Some of these modern chairs are ideal in kitchens because they are made of plastic or resin compounds and can be washed down if food is spilt on them. They can also be stacked so that, when they are not in use, they take up a minimal amount of space.

For breakfast bars and island units with an over-hang, high stools are the best type of seating, but these should be chosen with comfort in mind. The essentials for a good stool are a rail or foot bar and lumbar support for the lower back. High stools without a foot rail should be used only in conjunction with a bar or island unit that has an integral rail, otherwise the weight of the unsupported leg will restrict blood flow to the back of the thigh and cause discomfort. Lower lumbar or back support is also advisable to avoid the sitter slumping forward to support the upper torso or slouching. Good examples of well-designed stools are the Lem highstool by Shin and Tomoko Azumi for Lapalma and the Silver Bombo by Magis.

In small kitchens, foldaway chairs or stools might be most satisfactory. When not in use these can be stored in a cupboard or hung from a peg rail. In some situations, built-in benches or window seats can be useful, especially for families with a number of young children. Built-in seating is sturdy and attached to the wall so unlikely to rock or topple, and the base can be designed so that the seat is hinged and the space underneath used to store toys or outdoor clothes.

Below far left: Small areas can be configured to house a breakfast bar for snacks and informal meals; here a wide shelf surface is used in conjunction with two stylish tall chairs.

Below left: This seating has been chosen according to height and function: low chairs at the dining table and tall stools at the bar.

Below: Loose covers can transform a utilitarian chair into something grander for formal dining. Covers made from washable fabrics can be removed and laundered then replaced to maintain an immaculate appearance.

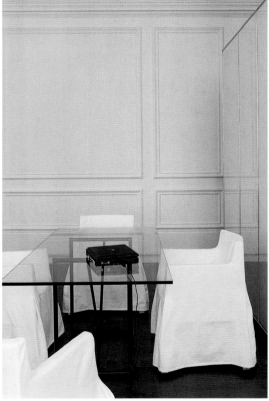

LIGHTING

Natural light is both the best and cheapest form of illumination to work by, so make the most of it in your kitchen. Keep blinds and curtains gathered well back from the window, and unless the view is unpleasant avoid cluttering up the windowsill with pots of utensils or cookery books. Also, paint the sill and surround of the window with white or a light-coloured paint so that the daylight will be reflected rather than absorbed, as it would be with a dark shade.

There are many ways of enhancing available daylight; for example, shiny surfaces such as steel and pale or white-faced units will reflect light and increase its impact. In a dark kitchen you could introduce more windows or add a glass panel to a door that has access to the outside, although for security reasons this door might need to be fitted with reinforced glass and a protective grille. If wall space is limited but roof access is available, you might introduce a glass dome into the ceiling, which will allow more daylight in. If you are considering extending your kitchen, incorporate a conservatory or use large sections of

Below: Good natural light is a real bonus in a kitchen, creating a pleasant working environment, but you will have to supplement it with task lighting focused on work surfaces and hobs.

Right: If daylight is scarce, make the most of what is available by using light colours, such as white, on the walls, and introducing reflective materials, such as stainless steel, on surfaces.

Below right: Recessed downlighters on dimmer switches are placed above this breakfast bar area; the lights can be used at full force when the bar is used for food preparation, but dimmed to a more moody and restful level for dining.

Left: There are no windows in this part of the kitchen, so, to compensate, every surface is gleaming white. A black ceramic hob breaks up this expanse of white, and its shape is echoed in the ceiling panel holding three spotlights directed over the working area. The shape of the spotlights is in turn picked up by the round handles on the unit doors.

Below left and below: The long glass cabinet that runs above the entire length of the work surface has been backlit to cast a soft yellow glow through the neatly aligned wine glasses contained in it.

NUTS AND BOLTS

Below: Daylight streams through the floor-to-ceiling window at one end of this kitchen, so the owner could choose dark colours for the surfaces. The upper units, though dark in colour, have an almost mirror-like finish, so they reflect the row of glass-shaded pendant lamps above the island unit.

Right: Glass shades allow the light to illuminate and bounce off the ceiling, as well as shine downwards.

Below right: This work area is positioned facing a good-sized window, but the light is supplemented with a pendant light. This area above the hob is prone to grease and steam, so the shade should be durable and easy to wipe clean.

glass panelling instead of or as part of a wall. All these large-scale projects should be done in consultation with an architect and structural engineer and may require planning permission from the local authority.

Even in kitchens with a good supply of natural light, supplementary artificial lighting is essential. Artificial or electric lighting can be divided into three sections – ambient, task and decorative.

Ambient light is the overall light that illuminates a room. It can be made up of a central ceiling light in conjunction with wall or side lights. This level of light should be of sufficient strength to allow you to see what you are doing while carrying out general tasks.

For more specific and detailed work you will need dedicated task lighting. This is especially important in a kitchen where sharp knives are used for cutting, hot pots and pans are placed to cook on flames or hot rings, and boiling liquids poured from one container to another. Direct lighting must be focused on certain

key working areas, such as the hob, the work surface and over the sink and draining board.

Task lighting should be positioned so that the beam shines directly on the intended surface. Do not rely on spotlights positioned on the ceiling to be sufficient for this as the beam from such a light will usually make first contact with the back of the person working at the surface beneath, and therefore cast a shadow over the area in front of them.

Decorative lighting can be part of the ambient lighting scheme, but will not in itself provide adequate overall illumination to work by. Decorative lights include wall lights in ornate shades, which cause the beam of light to be directed towards the ceiling, and side or table lights with colourful or patterned shades that glow attractively but provide a low level of light.

If the kitchen is part of a dining space, candles could be used in the evening. The candles should be arranged on or around the table for a romantic and flattering low-level light, but additional task lighting will be essential for any work being carried out.

Dimmer switches can be used to lower the level of brighter ambient or decorative lights. Such switches play a useful part in the overall illumination of a room because the level can be adjusted to that needed at any one time. Lights may be wired on various circuits so ambient and decorative lights, useful for evening entertaining or general relaxing, are on one circuit, whereas task and spot lights are kept on a separate circuit so they can all be turned off at once. When planning your kitchen lighting, make sure the light switches are positioned by the main door so that you do not have to stagger around the kitchen to find your way out when the lights have been turned off.

The kitchen is a damp and steamy place, so lights with electrical connections should be in sealed and damp-proof covers. This is especially important for lighting close to sinks and hobs, such as under-unit strip lights. The casing, or protective cover, should also be easy to wipe clean, so that when grease accumulates and starts to effect the strength of light being transmitted, it can be removed.

Top left: When you place individual lights together the beams overlap to create a single band of light when they hit the surface below.

Top centre: If you find an area needs a specific beam of light then a clip-on spot can be useful.

Above left: A smoothly curved wall light blends in with the white wall while the beam of the spotlight is directed onto the sink.

Above centre: Up-lighters recessed in the floor can be used to highlight structural features and create a feeling of height in a room.

Above: A small dining area is defined and highlighted by a ceiling light with a decorative shade, whose fluted shape echoes the wavy outline of the table.

The Personal Touch

INTRODUCTION

You can customize your kitchen with arrangements and displays of china, glass and smaller objects. These things will bring life and personality to the room and many of them will be useful as well as beautiful.

Although you refine your kitchen at each step of the building and fitting process with your choice of units, finishes and machines, it is the fine details that complete the process. Many of these small accessories will be selected in conjunction with things you have already or as a result of your lifestyle, and the type of cooking and the style of entertaining you enjoy. For example, the utensils you use might be dictated by the pans you have – non-stick pans require wooden or plastic utensils that won't damage the inner coating whereas cast-iron pots are hardy enough to

tiles and simple utensils, a vibrantly patterned curtain, tablecloth and cushions covers will lift the whole appearance. Soft furnishings can be useful for those who like to update and change the scheme seasonally or on a regular basis because the plain kitchen will provide a neutral background against which fashionable accessories can be placed.

The personal touch is not only about fashion and style, it is also about identifying things that really suit you, the gadgets you understand and work well with. These items might include a favourite small sharp

withstand use with metal implements. If you follow a certain decorative theme in your kitchen the china and glassware you select can endorse it – terracotta plates for a Mediterranean-inspired room or simple white china for a minimalist environment. In a family kitchen more decorative tableware or even colourful unbreakable crockery might fit the bill.

When it comes to fabrics and window treatments the materials you select can have a noticeable impact. For example, in a kitchen with pale yellow walls, matching plain units with chrome D handles, undecorated

knife that does a dozen jobs, from peeling to chopping, and never fails, or the wooden spatula that works for every occasion, from stirring soups to making sauces. Whatever you choose, remember that it is worthwhile investing time and money in selecting the best things you can (and this doesn't necessarily always mean the most expensive), because your kitchen and tableware are likely to be with you for some time to come. The priority is to select things that do their job with ease and are sturdy enough to put up with the wear and tear involved in daily kitchen life.

GADGETS AND UTENSILS

Let us start this section with a word of warning – gadgets can also be gimmicks, and at some time most of us will have been seduced into buying something that we didn't really need. Hidden in many kitchen drawers is the vegetable cutter that makes star shapes, bought at an in-store demonstration and used perhaps twice since its purchase. There might also be the toasted sandwich-maker that was great in student days but now gathers dust in a cupboard – both items are very much surplus to requirements.

Other items, such as deep-fat fryers, ice-cream, bread and yoghurt makers, are machines that should only be purchased if you are absolutely convinced that their useful life will last longer than the time it takes for a fashionable fad to pass. A lot of these machines are purchased because they represent a lifestyle we would like to have but don't have time to accommodate. There *are* people who bake their own bread every day and cultivate yoghurt on a regular basis. Ask yourself to which category you really belong.

Unnecessary or outdated gadgets and machines should be disposed of. It is a waste of valuable kitchen cupboard space to store them. If a gadget or utensil has not been used for more than two years then it is time for it to go. You will have been through the seasonal cooking cycle twice, and if you have not needed it in that time, then it is unlikely you will again. Certain items, such as numerical cake tins, large serving platters for parties and even fish kettles, can often be hired through a local bakery or cookery supply shop, so you may not need to invest in, or store them, in the first place.

When buying gadgets and utensils, don't allow yourself to be overwhelmed by glamour packaging and good sales patter. As a rule, the more dials and sockets there are, the more there is to go wrong. Once you have established the type of the machine you want, at the right price, then look at the manufacturer's name. In the long run, the established companies with affiliated suppliers are more likely to be around when you need repairs or replacement parts.

Left: A metal draining rack has a pleasingly functional appearance; this lightweight metal frame is practical but unobtrusive on the worktop.

Above: Utensils should be stored close to where they are to be used, but if they are to be on show try to make sure that they are clean and of a similar style or make so that there is visual uniformity. The selection of utensils shown here are hung from a simple metal rail from S-shaped hooks.

Right: When it stands alone on a gas ring a kettle becomes a point of interest; this round steel one is a focal point among a line of decorative glass bottles.

Above: A utensil holder with varied display heights keeps the spoons and ladles in one place, but also makes it easy to see and select what you need.

Below: This wooden breadboard has a removable slatted grille top that allows the breadcrumbs to fall through to collect in the base; there is also a recess in which the bread knife can be stored readily to hand but with the blade safely sheathed.

Below right: A purpose-designed knife block is heavy enough to sit comfortably at an angle that makes it easy to pull out individual blades and to allow for knives of different lengths to be stored. It also provides an interesting embellishment on a worktop, as do the attractive pepper grinder, oil drizzler and bowls.

Right: This specially designed knife drawer has a recess made to fit each knife in the battery. This storage protects the blades and makes them easily identifiable and accessible.

Most of the best gadgets and utensils are classics, those that carry on from generation to generation. These items survive and continue to be popular because they do the job they were designed to do, efficiently and effectively. That is not to say that some of the new designs and contemporary labour-saving innovations that flood the market each year aren't great, but much of the traditional basic kit makes a good foundation on which to build.

In the next few pages we look at some of the most popular and most enduring utensils and gadgets, discuss their uses and the best way of storing and maintaining them. This is an elementary guide; the final choice is up to you, and what suits your way of life.

BOARDS

Chopping boards protect the worktop beneath them and provide an easily transportable surface on which to prepare ingredients and take them to the pot or dish in which they will be cooked or served. Most chopping boards are simple flat surfaces, but there are those with a dropped and raised lip at either end. The lower lip fits over the edge of the work surface and prevents the board from slipping. The other end, with an upward lip, prevents items from falling off the board while chopping or moving them around. Other boards have a small trough around the edge to collect juices and other liquids, or a drawer underneath, the chopping surface forming a sliding lid.

Some kitchen manufacturers will supply boards specifically designed to fit over a sink or double-sink unit. This adds to the amount of work surface and allows washed produce, such as fruit and vegetables, to be taken directly from the adjacent sink to be prepared. The leftovers can then be thrown directly into the waste disposal unit, in or between the sinks, or into the bin underneath.

The old-fashioned butcher's block is also basically just a chopping board, but many modern designs come on a wheeled trolley base so that they can be rolled from one area to another. When in situ the wheels can be locked so that the block is stablized to become an additional work surface. In a large kitchen this can be an easy and effective way of transporting ingredients from the sink to the oven or hob if they are some distance apart.

Health and safety recommendations suggest different chopping boards be used for various tasks. For example, red meat should be prepared on a board dedicated to this type of meat; raw chicken is another product that should be prepared and stored using separate apparatus. Fish and garlic may also require their own board because of the strong odours that can linger. Whatever they have been used for, all boards and surfaces must be thoroughly cleaned after use.

Wood is by far the most common material used for chopping and bread boards, and it is believed to have a natural bacteria-killing property. Wooden boards can be washed with very hot water, but it is best not to use high-strength detergents. Reinforced glass and resin composites make good surfaces on which to chop fruits and vegetables as they are lightweight and also easy to wash. Marble is traditionally the surface chosen for making pastry because it is cold and pastry is best kept chilled before baking.

KNIVES AND BLADES

A good set of knives, varying in size from a small sharp paring knife to a serrated-edge bread knife and a carving knife, which has a long slightly flexible blade, is a necessity in a kitchen. Palette knives are useful if you bake, as they are smooth sided and can be used to spread ingredients, such as jam into a pie base or uncooked cake mix. For chopping fresh herbs there is a specific utensil with a curved blade and a handle at either end called a *mezzalune*; this can be used in a wooden or stone bowl or on a flat surface.

Most modern knives have stainless steel blades that retain their sharpness, but for the keen cook a non-stainless steel knife, which can be whetted or sharpened to a really fine edge, is an essential. Check the labels or packaging to see if knives can be put in a dishwasher, because some, such as non stainless steel blades, are best hand-washed and will require light oiling to prevent rust.

Knife storage is important for safety and ease of selection. Avoid storing them loose in a drawer or you will cut your fingers when removing one; arrange them according to size in a knife block or on a magnetic strip, close to where food preparation takes place.

Among other utensils with blades or cutting surfaces you will find that a good pair of sharp kitchen scissors is indispensible, as is a tin opener. A garlic press provides a quick and easy alternative to fine dicing with a knife and a hand grater can grate small amounts of food such as cheese or breadcrumbs when you don't want to use an electrical processor. A small vegetable peeler, which may also be used on fruits such as apples and pears, is another handy basic.

There are many pieces of more specialist equipment, such as a grapefruit knife, apple corer, egg slicer, nutmeg grater and poultry shears, but at this level of fine tuning it is up to you as an individual to decide what tools you think you will use regularly.

SPOONS AND LADLES

In some recipes measurements for small amounts of ingredients are often given by spoon size, such as teaspoon or tablespoon, and these regular items of cutlery are also handy for general cooking and baking requirements. For example, when putting a small amount of vanilla essence into cake mix you are less likely to make a mistake if you put the essence on to a spoon first rather than directly from the bottle into the mix. A tablespoon is useful for spooning out portions of meringue mix or individual helpings of mousse from a larger bowl,

so a couple of standard spoons are always useful and can be kept in a drawer or utensil pot on the work surface. A generous size basting spoon should be included, preferably one with a long handle so that your hand is well away from the heat source and splashes when pouring juices or fat over a roast. A perforated spoon, for draining vegetables and extracting eggs from boiling water, is helpful, as is a good size ladle when it comes to apportioning sauces and soups.

These larger spoons are often hung, along with a fish-slice, on a wall-mounted rail close to the hob or oven so that they are to hand when needed. If they are left on display then they should be uniform in style and finish, preferably in stainless steel or enamel.

SUNDRIES

A small portable timer is invaluable for keeping track of boiling pots. Most ovens come with an integral timer, but for pots and pans that need careful monitoring on the hob, a timer is invaluable.

Sieves and colanders for straining ingredients such as rice and pasta are also a basic requirement. The colander has small feet so that it can stand on its own, whereas the sieve, which usually has a finer mesh and a handle, is designed to be placed over the top of a saucepan or bowl. It can also be used to sift flour.

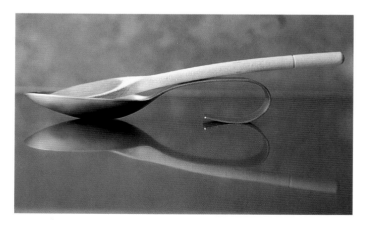

A measuring jug and weighing scales are vital for getting the right quantities of ingredients. Weighing scales come in several styles from the most modern with digital read-out to the old-fashioned, with small metal weights that have to be changed manually.

Waste bins are a necessity in a busy kitchen, and two or three might be required if recycling is part of your household routine. If possible, larger bins for materials to be recycled should be kept in a utility room and small quantities accumulated in a basket or box in the kitchen and then transported to the bin. Finally, a step ladder or step seat can aid access to upper shelves and cupboards.

ELECTRICAL APPLIANCES

The electric kettle has become a fashionable kitchen accessory. Its principal function of boiling water has not changed, but nowadays there are transparent styles so that you can watch the water bubble, cordless options that allow you to pick the kettle up unhindered and move it another place, and coloured and patterned ones that will coordinate with any style or shade of kitchen décor. The appearance of the kettle is significant, because it is used regularly and remains on the work surface. As it is visible it needs to be attractive; it also requires frequent wiping with a moist cloth to keep it clean.

Above: The single continuous rail that runs along this reflective splashback is used not only to keep kitchen paper and utensils readily to hand, but also as a display area. The well-selected pieces of equipment – ladle, fish slice, whisk and spatula, and so on – are in stainless steel and they have been arranged equidistant from each other, giving a pleasing symmetry. They are also all mirrored in the splashback, creating an unusual optical dimension.

Far right: This graceful metal spoon rest, itself simply a large spoon with its handle rolled under as a support, prevents drips of oils and gravy from mixing and serving spoons marking the work surface.

The food processor is a useful machine and in some cases it can incorporate the functions of several other pieces of equipment. For example, the grater disc can be used for cheese, carrots and other ingredients. But you might question whether it is worth the effort of retrieving the machine, if it is stored elsewhere, fitting it up with the correct blade and then washing the container, lid and blade, if the quantity of grated cheese you require is small. As mentioned above, the old-fashioned box grater can be best for smaller amounts, while the food processor is ideal for large quantities or if you are planning a baking session. Similarly, the processor will have a whisking option and perhaps even a juice extractor, but a small hand-held whisk is invaluable for whipping up sauces or beating an egg and a lemon squeezer can obtain juice from just a couple of citrus fruits.

THE PERSONAL TOUCH

The food processor is the modern version of the mixer, which is a steel bowl and an overhead arm into which two metal beaters are attached. This type of machine has had something of a revival and is part of a general movement favouring vintage equipment and styling. The mixer incorporates the style of machine introduced in the 1950s, but with modern updates and wiring. Blenders and toasters are also available with this type of retro feel.

The dilemma when it comes to storing electrical machines is that they are bulky, so are best stored off the worktop, where they take up a considerable amount of space, but they should be kept close to where they are most used or the effort of getting them out will put you off ever using them. The ideal place is behind a sliding panel or door or on a recessed section of worktop – the doors keep the machine out of sight and protect it from grease and splashes of food being prepared nearby. If you do not have sufficient storage space on or adjacent to the surface then place the machine under a wipe-clean cover. Many manufacturers supply these or you can make your own out of a piece of PVC or sturdy plastic.

Left: Chrome and stainless steel finishes will work in every setting because they reflect colour rather than dictate it.

Above: All electrical appliances invariably have plugs that require sockets, which can be ugly. Here a neatly bevelled mirrored panel, which matches the splashback, contains and disguises the socket. Mirror is a useful material because it can easily be wiped clean and will reflect light.

Below: There are classic designs in certain electrical goods that seem to endure. For example, this stainless-steel Duralit toaster is a vintage style still in production today. Its continuing appeal is such that it can be found on worktops and breakfast bars in houses and apartments all around the world – a tribute both to its obvious good looks and its efficient functionality.

Below: Frequently used items or interesting pieces of equipment, such as a coffee maker, can be arranged to create a focal point on a long run of featureless worktop. A fish kettle is only used from time to time, but it is an attractive object to display and it can be a useful place to store and contain smaller gadgets and utensils.

Right: A separate area of work surface away from the main run of worktop can be a good place to store and use a food proccessor, though if you do not use it on a regular basis it will need some sort of protective cover.

Personal preferences will also dictate whether you go down the route of having a coffee-maker. There are many different types of coffee machine available, from the simple two-jug dripping filter to dedicated espresso and cappuccino makers. The latter are usually left on the worktop because they are something of a fashionable status symbol, and the true coffee addict will use them on a daily basis to get their caffeine fix. But if your coffee machine is to be a feature on the work surface, then you must make sure unsightly spills and coffee grains are cleaned up from around the base.

POTS AND PANS

The type of pots and pans you use might be dictated purely and simply by the source of heat and the type of oven you use. If you have a solid-fuel range, heavy-base pans, such as cast iron and

Above: A range of shapes and sizes of pots and pans will cater for various types of cooking, but check the type of material they are made from and whether it suits your oven and hob. It can also be space saving to stack pots in one drawer and the lids separately on a shelf or in a narrower drawer.

Right: The bases of pots may become marked and blackened with use so line the drawer or shelf where they are stored with strong paper, or a metal or soft plastic sheet that can be replaced or washed from time to time.

cast aluminium, are best, especially for slow cooking. Gas hobs are usually solid and fairly durable in construction, so most stainless-steel, vitreous enamel or aluminium pots and pans are suitable. But on smooth glass-top or ceramic electric and halogen units you are restricted to pans with a light, smooth base if you want to avoid damaging the delicate surface of the hob.

Copper has long been a favourite material for saucepans in professional kitchens, as it conducts heat efficiently and uniformly. Copper pans are attractive, but they must be well polished if they are to be on show. Most pots and pans will become stained with use and age and are bulky, so they are kept out of sight in drawers or cupboards near the oven or hob. But some, such as colourful enamel-covered cast-iron casseroles, can contribute to the overall scheme of a French country style or a farmhouse-inspired room.

Below far left: When not in use these drinks coasters may be neatly stacked on their own metal stand. These simple black rounds would suit any setting.

Below left: Kitchen roll can be kept on a wall-mounted holder or upright on a work surface using a metal stand like this.

Bottom left: An old-fashioned ham slicer is a specialized machine. It can be used to cut most types of cooked meats, but it is primarily a professional machine and should be used with care in a domestic environment.

Below: For those who enjoy making soups and sauces, or for parents with young babies who need to purée small quantities of food, there is nothing like the traditional *mouli legume*, although a food processor gives a similar results.

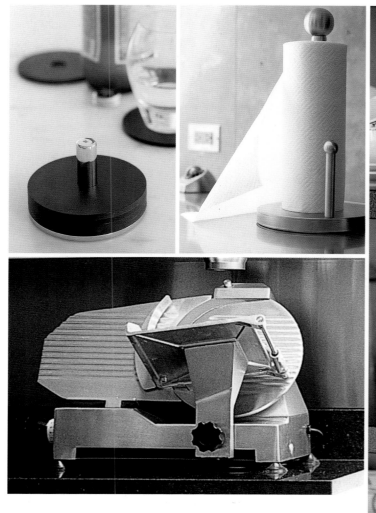

TABLEWARE

Your selection of tableware will be one of the most important parts of the personalizing process for your dining and kitchen areas. China and glassware should be chosen to suit your likes and dislikes in terms of colour and shape, as well as the type of food you regularly prepare, present and eat. It is also worth considering the fact that well-chosen plates and bowls can make a plain table look exciting, and might even help a bland meal seem more appealing. Physical

preferences also come into play; the shape and size of the handles on cups and cutlery are best chosen by actually holding and testing them. If you have large hands or long fingers, handles on cups and mugs need to be pronounced and generous rather than slimline and close to the body of the vessel, otherwise it can be difficult to pick the cup up without spilling the contents or burning your fingers.

CHINA AND CERAMICS

Contemporary tableware comes in many shapes and sizes, and has evolved with culinary trends and social changes. With the steady decline of the traditional 'meat and two veg' meal, the role of the standard dinner plate has slowly been usurped by the bowl, which can be used for soup, pasta, risotto or salad, as well as breakfast cereals and take-away meals such a chop-suey or noodle dishes.

Most households have more than one set of china; they might have a formal service that is used for special occasions, and an everyday set. But, increasingly, the formal service is being dropped in favour of what would more correctly be termed a plain service. In the past, the formal service was made of bone or fine china and had a border motif, often enhanced by a gilded line or over-pattern, around the rim of the plates and dishes. It was stored in the dining room or in a china cabinet in the eating area of an open-plan living room. Now the trend is to have undecorated china, often white, which can be set on a plain cloth with napkins and good glassware for the formal occasion, but also mixed with patterned and colourful

Left: The mostly white china and ceramics on show on these deep wooden shelves endorse the Mediterranean feel of the overall scheme of the room.

Above left: A collection of jugs can be a decorative feature in their own right, but they are also useful as containers for spoons and spatulas.

Above right: Attractive old flour and spice jars are very collectable.

Right: This custom-made dresser contains most of the china used every day in this family dining area. The china is a mix of both old and new, but all of the pieces have a similar plain white glaze finish so there is uniformity.

Main picture: White ceramics, whether they be storage vessels or tableware, will work in every setting and with most styles; you can add additional settings to a standard dinner service by mixing in extra white plates and bowls.

Inset: The appearance of food can be enhanced by the colour and style of dish on which it is presented. This vintage dessert plate with an ornate pink pattern picks up the rich colour of the fruit pie filling.

Right: Simplicity is the key to good presentation; overly ornate or fussy tableware can detract from the food being served on it.

ware for other times. This more functional tableware is generallly kept in the kitchen, either stacked on open shelves, where it becomes a simple but significant feature, or in cupboards near the table or the dishwasher where it is used and washed.

The advantage of a plain service is that it is a perfect background with which to mix and match glassware and other decorative pieces. For example, it could be mixed with small blue-and-white Oriental bowls for a Thai or other Asian meal, or with terracotta bowls for an Italian-themed evening. If it is going to be used regularly, it is a wise idea to buy the china from a standard, universally available range, so that if you break a piece you will be able to replace it easily.

The mixing and matching of tableware can be taken one step further. In some Eastern countries, there is a system of dressing a table known as Table Talk. Instead of setting each place in the same ware this approach advocates setting places with different china and glassware to reflect the character or interests of the person who will sit there. For example, someone with an affinity for water or a love of swimming could have a setting focused on the colour blue, another person with an interest in gardening could have a green plate with a fresh flower placed on his or her napkin.

Basic household china includes six of each of the following: side plates, soup/cereal bowls, pudding plates, dinner plates, plus two vegetable dishes, a serving plate and sauce or gravy boat. There is also a standard tea service, but in most homes the tea cup and saucer has been replaced by the mug, and teapots are no longer required when you can dunk a tea bag into a mug of hot water and brew up a single cup as and when you want it.

Odd items of china and ceramic ware that are useful but do not necessarily have to match any particular style or design include egg cups, and the salt and pepper or cruet set. But with the rising use of peppercorns and rock salt condiment grinders are more popular, and these tend to be of plastic, wood or steel rather than ceramic. A butter dish with a lid is handy, as are jugs in various sizes and capacities, for milk, fruit juice, gravy, sauces and dressings. Larger serving bowls, especially oven-proof dishes that can be used for both cooking and serving, are a bonus. This type of dish might be manufactured in oven-safe glass, which makes no design or colour statement so blends innocuously with any style of tableware

Good care of your crockery and ceramics will help prolong both their use and good appearance. Avoid knocking and banging these delicate items against harder surfaces, and do not subject them to extremes of temperature. Unless they are specifically manufactured

for oven use, do not place china or ceramics in a high-temperature environment as they will crack and break. Always make sure any decorated china is dishwasher proof before machine washing, as certain gilding and metallic finishes will tarnish, and some glazes on hand-made pottery will discolour. Also 'peasant' style tableware such as terracotta may be porous on unglazed areas and therefore unsuitable for immersing for prolonged periods in detergent.

CANDLESTICKS AND TABLE DECORATION

Candlesticks are another element of table dressing and general room decoration; they can be made of metal, but glass and china designs are also popular and generally less expensive. Candlelight is rarely sufficient to work by, but it can be used for decoration, to create a mellow level of light and enhance the mood of relaxation and enjoyment. In an open-plan kitchen, candlelight can also focus attention on the dining table, putting the rest of the kitchen and the food preparation areas in shadow once a meal has started. Tall traditional candlesticks, which hold a pillar or tapered candles, give

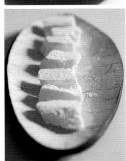

Left: Try to match the amount of food to the size of the dish. Oriental meals can often consist of several small portions rather than a single large helping.

Below left: Serving dishes and plates can be a different shape and style from the dining plates, and they can in some cases be chosen specifically to complement the food they are to carry.

Centre left: If possible, use cutlery that is suitable for the food; for example sushi and tempura are often eaten with chopsticks.

Below left: For a simple meal, such as sauasages, or for barbecues that are to be eaten outdoors, use everyday, inexpensive tableware.

Bottom left: Decorated china can be distracting, but for simple food such as rice or plain pasta it can add to the table setting.

Below: Plates should be sizeable enough to allow a diner to put shells, bone, rind, skin or skewers to one side, without interfering with the rest of the meal.

Right: Simple, unadorned finishes and clean shapes in ceramic and glassware are versatile enough to include in almost any style of table setting. Here they mix with ceramic-handled cutlery. Contemporary designs can have a similar appearance to that of old bone, but they are more able to withstand the high temperatures of a dishwasher cycle.

height and elegance to a table, whereas small glass votive holders that hold tealights bathe the cloth in a soft golden light. Wide ceramic bowls in which you can float specially made flat candles combine the opposing elements of fire and water, and scented candles may also add to the ambience, but they should be used sparingly in a place where food is prepared and served as a conflicting combination of aromas might be overpowering.

For outdoor entertaining such as barbecues, lanterns or candle holders that incorporate protective glass surrounds are helpful, especially when there is a breeze. Glass containers, such as sturdy hollow glass columns or tall vase-like shapes with sand in the bottom into which a thick church candle can be set, can be bought from most department stores.

STORAGE

Although not always made of china, storage jars and containers are included in this section because they are usually sold in the same shops or parts of department stores as the other items in this section. When choosing storage containers, select the size and type to suit the contents – for example, dried fruit can be quite sticky so use a plastic or glass container which is easily washed. Dried pulses and herbs must be stored in dry and air-tight container, so seek out those with a screw top or rubber seal. For tea, coffee and sugar, which are used frequently, containers should be easy to open and close and, if they are left out on a worktop, they should be in matching finishes.

GLASSWARE

Although measures have been taken to bring cut glass to a broader audience, with fashion designers such as John Rocha, Louise Kennedy and Jasper Conran creating ranges for internationally renowned manufacturers, the current trend is for unadorned, simple glassware rather than more ornate styles.

Glassware is an attractive feature on a shelf, as long as it is kept immaculately clean and shiny. A row of neatly stacked glasses on a gleaming stainless-steel or reinforced glass shelf can be highlighted by a well-placed directional spotlight. Coloured glasses, especially the hand-blown green-blue tumbler made from recycled glass, will bring a softer, less clinical look to a streamlined semi-professional setting.

Glasses come in a myriad of style and shapes, but the basic guideline is as follows. There are two sizes of wine glass: large and small. The smaller ones are generally used for white wine and the larger for red. Ideally, both types of wine glass should be large enough for there to be plenty of room to swirl the contents and release the aroma, and as a rule they shouldn't be filled beyond two-thirds capacity. Some people prefer a long-stemmed elegant shape in fine glass (some even believe that it improves the taste of the wine it holds), whereas others prefer a chunky tumbler with stable and solid contact with the table.

Wine glasses are traditionally set in a straight line across the top of the right-hand set of cutlery and in order of use – the white wine glass on the right, then one for red in the middle and a water glass following. But for informal dining, many people just have one glass for wine and another for water, whether for chilled tap water from a jug or mineral water from a bottle. Other popular glass types include larger beer or soft drink glasses, and a squat tumbler for spirits such as whisky. Among the more specialist types are the Martini or cocktail glass, sherry copitas, small liqueur and port glasses and the Brandy balloon.

Care of glassware is important to maintain its clear and sparkling appearance. Most glassware is best hand washed in warm water with a few drops of washing-up liquid. Rinse in cold water, allow to drain but not dry, and polish with a lint-free cloth – linen is often recommended. Glasses left to dry on a draining board inevitably get drip marks that dry to a cloudy streak. Rather than scrub marks baked on ovenproof glassware casseroles and dishes, leave them to soak in cool soapy water; scrubbing with a harsh abrasive such as wire wool can damage the surface. Never plunge a hot glass or ceramic dish straight into cold water as this will also cause them to break.

Left: There are several different styles and shapes of glasses, each of which is suited to a particular type of wine or drink. Long-stemmed glasses like these are usually used for wine, with the larger bowls for red and the smaller ones for white.

Below left: Because of its highly reflective properties glass can be very beautiful and it is often left on display; here three water carafes are aligned on a mantelpiece.

Below: Texture and feel can be as important as the shape or finish of tableware. This ribbed water carafe complements beautifully both the basketweave of a raffia underplate and the crisp white waffle-weave napkin, while the modern smooth, square ceramic napkin ring sets off the more stylized outline of the traditional knife and fork. The glossy finish of the table surface highlights the elegance of this monochrome grouping perfectly.

Bottom left: A separate water glass is usually provided so the wine glass need not be emptied before water can be taken. Coloured glass is a good choice with Eastern-style table settings as it is robust enough to stand up to the stronger colours usually used in this type of ware.

Below: If you entertain regularly it is worthwhile having specialized glasses, such as these elegant long-stemmed 1920s style cocktail glasses.

Right: Cut crystal is decorative and luxurious, and many of the styles and decorative patterns, such as those seen here combined with a modern clear glass water carafe, date back to the Georgian and Victorian eras. Glassware should always be immaculately clean; in hotels and formal dining rooms people setting the table with glasses traditionally wear lint-free cotton gloves to avoid putting greasy finger marks on the glass.

THE PERSONAL TOUCH

CUTLERY

You can acquire cutlery in many ways. Traditionally, the newly wed couple would be given a formal canteen as a wedding present to form a key part of their household apparatus. The canteen is a wooden box lined with felt or velvet and each piece of cutlery is set in its own niche. These days, most people start out by buying a six-person boxed set of cutlery and add to it as and when they need to.

It is common to have one style of cutlery, which can be cleaned in the dishwasher, for everyday use, and a more elaborate set for dinners and special occasions. The formal table setting of the last century often had bone- or ivory-handled knives, but in these more ecologically minded times they are no longer favoured, and a cream solid set plastic material is substituted in their place.

With the increasing interest in more diverse foods the standard knife, fork and spoon setting is not always the norm. Italian meals such as pasta are often served with a fork and a spoon, Oriental

dishes with chopsticks and risotto and other rice recipes with just a fork. Some Indian meals are simply eaten using the hands and a piece of bread which acts as a spoon-like scoop.

An everyday selection of cutlery should be based around six of each of the following: table knives, table forks, dessert forks, dessert spoons, dessert knives, soup spoons, tea spoons and two serving spoons. Extra specific formal pieces, such as fish knives and forks and steak knives and forks are not necessary, and their use has mainly gone out of fashion in the home, although they might still be placed on the tables in hotels and restaurants.

Everyday cutlery is usually kept in a sub-divided kitchen drawer. The division may be an integral part of the drawer or be a separate container bought specifically for the purpose. The divider should contain a small compartment into which each of the different types of knives, forks and spoons can be placed, with the smallest of the division reserved for teaspoons. This order makes it easy to identify and remove the right pieces of cutlery when laying the table.

More formal cutlery is usually silver or sliverplated, and may be referred to as silverware or flatware. It is often sold in canteens and in settings for six, eight or twelve people. There are several classic designs such as Rattail, which has a raised central line on its handle and a rounded end. Fiddle is another traditional style and is named for its flattened shape and profile which is similar to the outline of a violin. Bead is similarly called after its design, which features a raised dot or bead-like pattern around the edge of the handle.

Far left: The colourful red handles of this spoon and fork are in keeping with the vintage print tablecloth and the enamelled dish.

Above left: Contemporary cutlery designs are usually simple and unadorned, but the shapes and finishes are often interesting.

Right : To store formal silver or silver-plated cutlery it is best to have a dedicated drawer, preferably lined with a soft cloth or felt to prevent scratching.

ARTWORK AND DECORATIVE DETAILS

As has been said often in this book, the kitchen is a place where steam, moisture and grease are daily by-products. These elements have an accumulative and sometimes damaging effect, so this is not an ideal location for valuable artworks, but you can decorate walls with framed posters and photographs, ceramics and other objects.

CLOCKS

A good size, easy-to-read wall clock is an accessory often found in kitchens, not so much for timing individual pots and dishes, as these are usually covered by the oven timer or separate mobile timer, but for overall time keeping. As a wristwatch is often removed when working in the kitchen, a wall clock enables you, at a glance, to keep track of meal times and when you need to go to collect children from school or how much time is left until guests arrive for dinner.

Left: A clock, like a painting, can stand out as a decorative feature in what is an otherwise plainly decorated room. Most wall-mounted clocks are battery operated so do not require any special electrical work to install.

Inset left: A clear, easy-to-read clock face is a help when it comes to timing the readiness of meals and keeping an eye on guest's arrival time.

Above: Although contemporary designer clocks are easily available and have modern movements, old and antique clocks have the special patina of age and an intrinsic style. Old railway station clocks and those used in public spaces such as department stores or shops can be attractive.

Above: This huge bright cartoon-style 1950s poster of the Sunbeam bread girl complements the vintage-style décor and colour theme of this kitchen. This location, directly above the hob, will attract a lot of grease and steam, so it should be reserved for the less precious pieces from your art collection.

Because the clock is usually wall mounted, the face and numerals need to be clean, uncomplicated and easy to view at a distance. This type of clock can be electric or battery operated; if it is electric it will need to be positioned near a socket and you will need to find a way of hiding trailing wires, which look ugly and can be dangerous. If the clock is battery operated, make sure that you can access it easily, even if you need the help of a step ladder, so that you can change the batteries when needed.

The clock should be sealed or in a well-fitting casing because steam, moisture and grease will rise and settle on it. Moisture could affect the mechanism of the clock, and the face will need to be wiped clean from time to time to keep the numbers clearly visible.

PICTURES AND POSTERS

If you have a painting that you want to hang in a kitchen area, place it as far away as possible from the hob, oven, grill and sink, where most of the adverse conditions originate. If your chosen picture is an oil painting then, in most cases, the surface should be left open, but any other medium – watercolour, acrylic, pastel or crayon drawing – will need to be protected under a glass covering.

Posters and photographs will also require framing under glass if you want them to last. If un-framed, a paper poster will become baggy and wrinkled from the moisture in the air, and photographs will become similarly bowed and bent. As the kitchen is generally used as a family room it can be a good place in which to display a range of photographs of family and friends or holiday locations. These can be arranged in a collage of cut-outs and overlaid prints, or if you have a good image it could be enlarged and made into a feature.

The surface of ceramic plates and glass dishes are designed to withstand heat and water, so they can be used successfully as a wall decoration. A plate from an old family dinner service or a series of hand-painted dishes from a foreign location can be secured in a wire frame that grips around the rim of the plate or dish and is then hung from a hook on the wall. Ceramic decorations can easily be taken down and, after the removal of the wire hanger, put in the dish-washer and washed so that they look clean and fresh.

NOTICE BOARDS

Notice boards are a useful addition to a kitchen: they can be places where shopping lists are kept and updated, where appointment cards are pinned as a reminder and, if located by the telephone, the site for a list of emergency phone numbers.

Ideally the pin or notice board should be positioned at eye-level or slightly above, and it can be fixed to a wall, back of a door or the side panel of an upper section of a storage unit. There are many types of notice board, from the classic cork panel with wood frame to the modern white board on which you write with a pen and wipe clean with a damp sponge. (These boards are not very practical for shopping lists, though, as the list would have to be transcribed onto paper.) Blackboards are an old-fashioned teaching aid, but can also have a place in the modern kitchen. Blackboard paint enables you to transform a smooth-surfaced panel, which can be free standing or be an integral part of a piece of furniture, into a blackboard. The disadvantage is that the chalk used to write on it creates dust, but if not close to a food preparation area this will not be a major problem.

Left above and below: Kitchens tend to be family rooms and arrangements of photographs and drawings, or pictures by friends and children, can be grouped to form a decorative panel on a plain wall. The variety of size and shape of the artworks adds interest, and as the photographs and drawings tend not to be valuable, standard clip frames and inexpensive borders are adequate. This style of arrangement can also be updated or added to.

Below: Three small blackboards provide a useful place to chalk up menus, reminders and shopping lists. Wipeable white boards are also an option.

FABRICS AND WINDOW TREATMENTS

Because the kitchen and the combined kitchen-dining room are both busy working environments, where cooking smells, moisture and grease are prevalent, there are some materials best avoided altogether, or used only in small cushion-size quantities. The best guide is to focus on materials that will machine-wash easily, and to avoid those such as velvet, tweed, felt and corduroy, which require dry cleaning. These thicker, denser fabrics will also absorb odours more, and if they are dark in colour they might also soak up light.

In the main, the fabric element of the decoration of any kitchen will focus on the windows, but in a kitchen-dining area, or a kitchen-family room combination, it will also cover the cushions and table linen such as cloths, napkins and place mats.

WINDOW TREATMENTS

In a kitchen, it is very important to make the most of any natural light available, but you might find you need to strike a balance between allowing plenty of light in and providing yourself with some privacy. If your kitchen window looks into your neighbour's home or over a dull brick wall, then you might prefer to obscure that view, but without obliterating the light altogether. This can be done with self-adhesive film that is applied directly to the glass, so it can still be used in

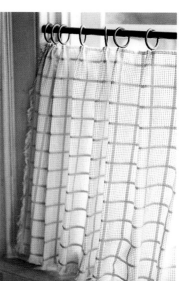

Far left: A lightweight voile curtain has been hung to follow the deep curve in the wall of this dining area. The curtains provide softness and some privacy, but don't cut out too much of the daylight.

Left: Half or café curtains add a pretty touch and can be used to cover the lower part of a window.

Above: Simple tabard-like fabric panels can be hung from hooks and loops to cover smaller windows or individual door panels.

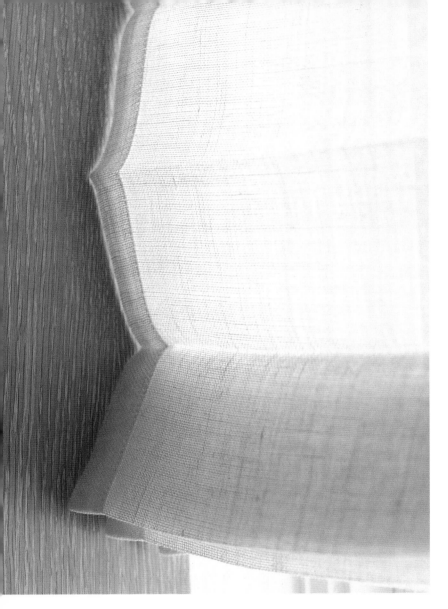

conjunction with curtains. The film comes in many forms, including an opaque finish that looks like sandblasted glass, a clear version with printed patterns, as well as gem-coloured sheets. If you have artistic leanings, and it is appropriate to the style of your kitchen, it can be interesting to create your own stained-glass effect by using strips or squares of different coloured film.

If your window has a deep frame or recess you could fill it with plastic drawer dividers. These come in cell sections, and they are intended for storing individual pairs of rolled-up sock or items of underwear. They are quite cheap and they can be found in good department stores as well as specialist storage shops. With a sharp pair of scissors you will be able to cut excess sections off so that the dividers slot neatly into the window frame creating a honeycomb effect. As they are plastic they are also easy to wipe clean.

CURTAINS

Fine cotton voiles and muslin curtains will also allow light through, but will create a hazy barrier between you and the world beyond the window. In a busy working kitchen this sort of treatment needs to be kept as close as possible to the window – you do not want loose fabric flapping into the washing-up water or billowing over the open flames of a burning hob. To create a curtain that will hang neatly flush to the window, you can sew narrow full-width pockets at each end of the fabric and thread through a fine wire or curtain pole. The wire can be fixed to the top and bottom of the window frame with small hooks, or a pole could rest on semi-circular cup fittings.

Café-style half-curtains give a European feel to a window and create a certain amont of privacy while still allowing light to stream in through the upper part of the window. Traditionally this type of

Above: Flat-folding fabric blinds fit neatly within the window frame and do not take up extra space. This type of blind can be pulled up to the very top of the window to allow the maximum amount of daylight into the room. When pulled down the fine linen material diffuses and softens the light.

Right: These fine laminated finish blinds have a soft sensuous handle, but they are easily wiped clean.

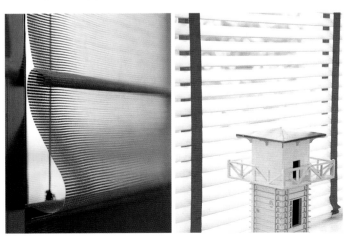

curtain, known as a *brise-bise* in France, is made from lace, but it can be created from various light-weight fabrics. The idea can also be updated as a length of coloured Perspex panel or as a series of banner-style sections of canvas.

BLINDS

Blinds are an excellent option for the window dressing in a kitchen because they fit neatly into the frame or surround of the window and can be pulled up and down, or folded back as needed. There are many different types of blinds you can choose from, but, as always for the kitchen, the most simple version is best.

Roller blinds are the most basic of the blind options. They are usually fitted to the top of the window so that they can be pulled down in front of the glass, and when not in use, rolled back up to the top where they obstruct only a minimal amount of light.

Roman blinds are raised and lowered by means of strips of cord or tape sewn along the back of the material. When pulled up they form neat overlapping pleats and when down they form a single flat panel. This type of blind has a pleasant appearance and can be made in voile-like materials, a printed cotton or softly-textured linen with a contrasting coloured band running around the edges. For a smarter treatment, the top may be concealed behind a pelmet.

Festoon and Austrian blinds are not really suitable for use in kitchens because they have numerous drapes and folds of fabric that act as grease traps and they tend to intrude beyond the frame of the window when furled or drawn up.

Venetian blinds control the direction and amount of light entering the room. The louvres or panels can be arranged to hang vertically or horizontally, but horizontal blinds are really only suitable for larger windows and areas such as French doors. New materials and finishes have brought Venetian blinds back into fashion; they can be bought ready made or made-to-order for a particular space, and with narrow, medium or wide slats. This type of blind operates by cords; one set pivots the louvres forward or back and another draws the whole blind up so that the window is unobscured. Venetian blinds are available in plastic, metal and wood.

Louvres and shutters can give a colonial feel to a room and will fold back neatly in jointed and hinged segments to give full access to the window. Half-window shutters can be fitted to the bottom section of a window to obscure the view, but leaving the top open to daylight. The unfussy lines of louvred shutters means that they work well with both simple and more decorative schemes.

Left: Standard louvre blinds are given impact by a bright red tape finish; the contrasting colours were specifically chosen to complement the punchy colour scheme in the rest of the room. Louvre blinds come in many colours and finishes, from wood to metal and from matt black to brilliant bronze.

Above: Dining spaces that are a part of, or adjacent to, the kitchen may require a more formal and decorative window dressing, especially if the area is used for dinner parties. Here, the graceful arches of the window frames create an interesting shadow beyond generously proportioned voile curtains.

be tied or attached to the seats by means of tapes or cords. Attach small piece of elastic at the end that is sewn to the cushion and this will provide a certain amount of flexibility.

TABLE LINENS

There are trends and fashions in tablecloths versus mats, but it comes down to personal taste and the state of the table top on which you intend to dine. For most family meals a polished or sealed wood, glass or resin tabletop is adequate and easy to wipe clean afterwards, although individual raffia, platicized or laminated mats may be introduced to protect the immediate surface area.

A cloth will always add a feeling of style and luxury to a table. The classic choice is white linen or cotton, but coloured tablecloths can be fun and used to endorse the decoration of the room or the type of meal being served. For example, a red-and-white gingham cloth will look great on a table set for an Italian-style supper party and a brightly coloured Provençal paisley print cloth will set the tone for an evening of dining on French bouillabaisse.

Linen or cotton table mats set on a polished wood table or a shining glass surface also look smart, and they are relatively easy to wash and launder, taking less ironing that a whole table cloth. Other materials such as slate and rubber are seen in mat form on more style-conscious tables, but these materials will not work well with classic formal plates and cutlery. Very simple white or contemporary china is best with these more unusual finishes.

Mats or a banner-style cloth will be the most useful form of table dressing for a breakfast bar or island dining area. The banner is a

CHAIR COVERS AND CUSHIONS

On a day-to-day basis, covers on kitchen chairs are probably more of a hindrance than a blessing, as they will quickly become soiled. However, removable slipcovers are very useful when you want to transform basic utilitarian seating into more attractive dining chairs. Upholstered cushions will give additional comfort and decorative interest to seats, benches and stools in a kitchen. Cushions should

Above: Simple canvas director's chairs can be dressed with tailored slipcovers for more formal occasions. If space is limited the chairs can be folded up and stored in a cupboard.

Right: Runners are increasingly popular, whether used as a centre panel on a polished wood or glass table, over a more formal full-sized cloth, or in bands across the table. They can be made in a variety of materials and in a range of bright colours which will add impact to any style of table dressing.

Left: Vintage and traditional table cloths can be found in antique shops and car boots sales.

Right and far right: In this bar area, where space is limited, three button-over hessian panels have been used to conceal the contents of the shelves behind. These panels can be easily lifted whereas a solid door would require space to open

simple broad strip of fabric that has been edged all the way round. For special occasions, the ends of a banner may be tapered and finished with a tassel or similar ornate decoration.

UTILITY LINENS

Tea towels and oven gloves are also an indispensible part of the kitchen linen closet. They can be in plain classic style or decorative, to co-ordinate or contrast with the room's overall scheme, and can be changed cheaply and easily. The use of tea towels has declined since the arrival of dishwashers, but they are still needed for drying good glasses and heavier pots and pans.

Oven gloves can be single gauntlet protectors or mitts at either end of a broad band of cloth. As oven gloves become grubby quite quickly make sure they are machine washable. Try not to hang oven gloves and towels on the handle or rail on the front of the oven door because they can, inadvertently, become wedged in the door and cause the oven temperature to drop; also the fabric may catch fire. The best place is to hang them from a rail or hook close by the oven.

Suppliers

SURFACES

Amtico
PO Box 42, Kingfield Road, Coventry
0800 667766 for stockists
www.amtico.co.uk
an extensive range of vinyl floor tiles, also laser-cut design service

Attica
543 Battersea Park Road, London SW11
020 7738 1234
specialists in stone tiles

Alfred McAlpine Slate
Penrhyn Quarry, Bethesda
Bangor, Gwynedd, Wales
01248 600656
specialists in natural slate tiles

Bushboard
01933 224 983 for stockists
splashback and worktop panels in brushed aluminium and some plain colours

Corres Tiles
Lichfield Terrace, Sheen Road
Richmond, Surrey
020 8332 9262
traditional and contemporary style of terracotta tiles

Criterion Tiles
196 Wandsworth Bridge Road
London SW6
020 7736 9610
terracotta, limestone and marble tiles

Dalsouple
PO Box 140
Bridgewater, Somerset
01984 667551 for stockists
modern rubber floor tiles

Domus Tiles
33 Parkgate Road, London SW11
020 7091 1500
ceramic flooring in matt and glazed finishes

Eight Inch
020 7503 3400 for suppliers
Tura glass and resin recycled composite surface 85 per cent recycled glass mixed with solvent free resins

Elon Tiles
66 Fulham Road, London SW3
020 7460 4600
www.elon.co.uk
hand-made tales from Europe and South America

Farbo-Nairn
PO Box 1, Kirkaldy, Fife 01592 643777
major suppliers of linoleum

Fired Earth
01295 812088 for branches around UK
limestone, slate, terracotta, ceramic, sandstone, mosaic and encaustic tiles

Forgetec
Scatterford Smithy, Newland
Coleford, Gloucestershire
01594 835363
patterned stainless-steel and aluminium flooring cut to size or in standard sheets

Harvey Maria
Trident Business Centre, 89 Bickersteth
Road, London SW17
020 8516 7788 for stockists
decorative cork tile with photo images of pebbles, roses and water

Jaymart Rubber & Plastics
Woodland Trading Estate, Eden Vale Road
Westbury, Wiltshire
01373 864926
rubber flooring in tiles and on the roll

Kirkstone Quarries
Skelwith Bridge, Ambleside, Cumbria
01539 433296
www.kirkstone.co.uk
specialists in riven and smooth slate tiles

Mega Marble
020 7372 1591 for sockists
www.megamarble.co.uk
marble specialist

Pallam Precast
187 West End Lane, London NW6
020 7328 6512
terrazzo floor tiles

The PhotoTile Company
2 Podmore Road, London SW18
020 8877 3733
www.phototile.co.uk
will transfer photographs onto tile

Pyrolave UK
0800 169 2374 for stockists
www.pyrolave.com
*volcanic stone base with a wide range of
coloured glaze coverings*

Rustica
154c Milton Park, Abingdon, Oxon
01235 834192
specialists in terracotta tiles

Siesta Cork Tile Company
Unit 21, Tait Road, Croydon, Surrey
020 8683 4055
cork tiles

Steristeel
0141 551 0707 for stockists
*stainless-steel splashbacks and work
surfaces*

Whitehall Fabrications
0113 2223000 for stockists
www.whitehall-uk.com
granite and Corian work surfaces

Wincanders
Amorim House, Star Road, Partridge
Green, Horsham, West Sussex
01403 71001
www.wincanders-amorim.co.uk
*wide range of cork flooring plus border and
design cutting service*

Vitruvius
20 Ransome Dock, 35 Parkgate Road,
London SW11
020 7223 8209
www.vitruvius.co.uk
stone and marble flooring

CABINETS
B&Q
0800 444840 for branches
*wide range of kitchen units, including
contemporary lines*

Boffi kitchens through Alternative Plans
9 Hester Road, London SW11
020 7228 6460
www.alternative-plans.co.uk
*a very versatile range allowing mix-and-
match styles and finishes*

Bulthaup
37 Wigmore Street, London W1
020 7495 3663
www.bulthaup.com
high-spec high-quality modern design

Chalon
The Plaza, 535 Kings Road,
London SW10
020 7351 0008
or 01458 2546000 for further stockists
www.chalon.com
classic and country style designs

Ikea
020 8208 5602 for branches
wide range of units, handles and surfaces

Kitchen Clinic
102–104 Shepherds Bush Road, London
W6 and 149 St Johns Hill, London SW11
020 7348 0877
www.kitchenclinic.com
helpful modern design team

Poggenpohl
0800 243781 for stockists
www.poggenphol.de
classic and contemporary designs

Plain and Simple
020 7731 2530
www.plainandsimple.com
many natural and wood-finished units

Roundhouse Design
25 Chalk Farm Road, London NW1
020 7428 9955
www.roundhousedesign.com
*bespoke cabinets and furniture from
classic to contemporary*

APPLIANCES
AEG
0870 5350 350 for stockists
*multi-function cookers including integrated
steam functions*

Aga Rayburn
08457 125207 for stockists
www.agarayburn.co.uk
*traditional style, enamel-front cast-iron
cookers*

American Appliance Centre
020 8443 9999 for stockists
*importer of major American brands,
including large refrigerators*

Brandt
01256 308000 for stockists
www.brandt.com/uk
*wide range of cookers and hobs including
a five-burner unit with central wok ring*

Buyers & Sellers
0845 085 5585
*leading discount suppliers for most
electrical kitchen machines*

De Dietrich
01256 308000 for stockists
*range of cookers including multi-function
oven with microwave and steamer oven*

Gaggenau
01780 722144 for stockists
www.gaggenau.com
many built-in appliance including ovens

Kuppersbuch
01257 270022 for stockists
www.kueppersbisch.de
*wide range of well-priced appliances
including two-level microwave system*

Neff
0870 513 3090
www.neff.co.uk
*cookers and extractor hoods including
the thermostatic flame-failure sensor for
gas hobs and cookers which registers
when a flame has gone out and shuts off
the gas supply*

Smeg
0870 4424465
www.smeguk.com
*makers of most electrical kitchen
machines, including the retro-style FAB
fridge with freezer box*

Sub Zero and Wolf
020 8443 9999 for stockists
*also available through leading retailers
including Allders, Harrods, Selfridges
and John Lewis stores
range of American refrigerators from
Sub-Zero, and cooking ranges from its
sister company Wolf*

SINKS AND TAPS
Atriflo
01708 526361 for stockists
www.avilion.co.uk
*stainless-steel kitchen tap collection
including streamline modern designs*

Franke
0161 436 6280 for stockists
taps and stainless-steel sinks

CP Hart
Newnham Terrace
Hercules Road
London SE1
020 70902 1000
*comprehensive selection of taps and
spouts*

Ideal Standard
01482 346461 for stockists
www.idealstandard.co.uk
*makers of Clear Tap, which incorporates
a filter*

Lansdowne
Elon Ltd
66 Fulham Road
London SW3
brochure line 020 8932 3966
www.kitchensinks.co.uk
*ceramic sinks and metal taps in traditional
styles*

Aston Matthews
020 7226 7220 for stockists
for taps and sinks

Villeroy and Boch
01291 650743 for stockists
brass and ceramic sinks

FREESTANDING FURNITURE
Ligne Roset
0845 6020267
www.ligne-roset.com
*freestanding cabinets, also shelving, tables
and seats*

The Conran Shop
Michelin House
81 Fulham Road
London SW3
020 7589 7401
www.conran.co.uk
*contemporary and ethnic cupboards; also
good for seating and tableware*

Habitat
0845 601 0740
www.habitat.co.uk
*wide range of contemporary cabinets,
furniture and lighting*

SCP
135–139 Curtain Road
London EC2
020 7739 1869

*Seating and storage; retailers of leading
contemporary designers such as Matthew
Hilton and Terence Woodgate, also classic
re-editions by Corbusier, Eames, etc.*

LIGHTING
Schott Fibre optics (UK)
01302 361574
*for fibre-optic installations to create special
effects in glass worktops and splashbacks*

Noel Hennessy
020 7323 3360
www.noelhennessy.com
*contemporary designs by many leading
European designers*

Purves & Purves
80–81 & 83 Tottenham Court Road
London W1
020 7580 8223
www.purves.co.uk
*wide range of lighting, also seating and
utensils*

Christopher Wray Lighting
199 Shaftesbury Avenue
London W1
and branches
020 7836 6869
www.christopher-wray.co.uk
wide range of task and decorative lighting

Photographic credits

l=left r=right b=below
a=above c=centre

2 Jamie Drake's apartment in New York; 3 a house in London designed by Gordana Mandic of Buildburo; 4–5 main pic Tristan Auer's apartment in Paris; 6–7 Penny Duncan's kitchen in London; 8–9 Sarah Featherstone's kitchen in London; 10–11 Kristiina Ratia's Connecticut home; 12 Sara & Joe Farley's apartment in New York, designed by Asfour Guzy; 13l Keith & Cathy Abell's New York house designed by 1100 Architect; 13r a house in London designed by Nico Rensch; 14–15 Sally Mackereth & Julian Vogel's house in London, designed by Wells Mackereth; 15a Marta Ventos' apartment in Barcelona; 15c Sally Mackereth & Julian Vogel's house in London, designed by Wells Mackereth; 15b Deirdre Dyson's home in London, kitchen by Bulthaup; 16bl a house in the Hamptons designed by Solis Betancourt; 16bc Kristiina Ratia's Connecticut home; 16br Beatrice de Lafontaine's kitchen in Knokke, designed by John Pawson; 17 Dominique Kieffer's apartment in Paris; 18–21 Beatrice de Lafontaine's kitchen in Knokke, designed by John Pawson; 22–25 A house in the Hamptons designed by Solis Betancourt; 26–27 Laurence Kriegel's apartment in New York; 28–31 Kristiina Ratia's Connecticut home; 32–33 Dominique Kieffer's apartment in Paris; 34–35 Gerhard Jenne's house in London, designed by Azman Owens Architects; 36–37 an apartment in Paris, designed by Abstrakt Architects; 38–41 Marina and Ivan Ritossa's 'Boffi' kitchen in London, designed by Alternative Plans; 42–45 Gerhard Jenne's house in London, designed by Azman Owens Architects; 46–47 Dean Smith & Pearl Wou's home in London; 49 Maria Reyes Ventos' apartment in Barcelona; 50–53 Richard & Lucille Lewin's house in London designed by Seth Stein; 54–55 Majid & Atsuko Sadaghiani's house in London, designed by Susanne Mahdavi of MK Architects; 56–59 an apartment in Paris designed by Frédéric Méchiche; 60–61 Sophie Douglas of Fusion Design & Architecture's converted barn in Somerset; 62–63 Catherine Chermayeff & Jonathan David's apartment in New York, designed by Asfour Guzy; 64–67 a house in London designed by Lynne Fornieles of Febo Designs; 68–69 an apartment in London designed by Gordana Mandic of Buildburo; 70–73 Mr & Mrs Moscowitz' Kitchen designed by Vicente Wolf; 74–77 Catherine Chermayeff & Jonathan David's apartment in New York, designed by Asfour Guzy; 78 Tony Baratta's house in Long Island; 79 Todd & Amy Hase's Bridgehampton house; 80–83 Angela Carr's house in London, designed by Azman Owens; 84–87 Evi Kalogianni Bouras' kitchen in London, designed by Adjaye & Associates; 88–91 an apartment in Belgium designed by François Marcq Flirte, kitchen designed by Fahrenheit; 92–95 Tony Baratta's house in Long Island; 96–99 Mr & Mrs Forrester's kitchen, designed by Johnny Grey; 100–101 Deirdre Dyson's home in London, kitchen by Bulthaup; 101a Marina and Ivan Ritossa's 'Boffi' kitchen in London, designed by Alternative Plans; 104l an apartment in Paris designed by Frédéric Méchiche; 104ar Sophie Douglas of Fusion Design & Architecture's converted barn in Somerset; 104br a house in the Hamptons designed by Solis Betancourt; 105a a house in the Hamptons designed by Solis Betancourt; 105b Mr Burke's kitchen designed by Courtney Sloane and Alternative Design; 106a Deirdre Dyson's home in London, kitchen by Bulthaup; 106–107 Laurence Kriegel's apartment in New York; 107a and b Mr & Mrs Van Hool's kitchen designed by Claire Bataille & Paul Ibens Design; 108ar Gerhard Jenne's house in London, designed by Azman Owens Architects; 108bl Peter Wheeler & Pascale Revert's London home, designed by Eric Gizard; 109bl Gerhard Jenne's house in London, designed by Azman Owens Architects; 110 Mark and Cynthia Wilkinson's kitchen in Wiltshire; 111a a house in London designed by Lynne Fornieles of Febo Designs; 111b a house in London designed by Nico Rensch; 112–113 Mr & Mrs Forrester's kitchen, designed by Johnny Grey; 114al Marta Ventos' apartment in Barcelona; 114ac Suzanne Tick & Terry Mowers' apartment in New York; 114ar Kristiina Ratia's Connecticut home; 114b Maria Reyes Ventos' apartment in Barcelona; 114–115 A house in New York designed by Shelton, Mindel & Associates; 115a Gerhard Jenne's house in London, designed by Azman Owens Architects; 115b Mr & Mrs Forrester's kitchen, designed by Johnny Grey; 116l Beatrice de Lafontaine's kitchen in Knokke, designed by John Pawson; 116ac Mr & Mrs Forrester's kitchen, designed by Johnny Grey; 116bc Deirdre Dyson's home in London, kitchen by Bulthaup; 116r Penny Duncan's kitchen in London; 117a Suzanne Tick & Terry Mowers' apartment in New York; 117b Sarah Featherstone's kitchen in London; 118l Catherine Chermayeff & Jonathan David's apartment in New York, designed by Asfour Guzy; 118c Mr & Mrs Van Hool's kitchen designed by Claire Bataille & Paul Ibens Design; 118r Maria Reyes Ventos' apartment in Barcelona; 119l Mr & Mrs Forrester's kitchen, designed by Johnny Grey; 119c Maxime & Athénais d'Angeac's home in Paris; 119r Sara & Joe Farley's apartment in New York, designed by Asfour Guzy; 120–121 Mark and Cynthia Wilkinson's kitchen in Wiltshire; 122al Sally Mackereth & Julian Vogel's house in London, designed by Wells Mackereth; 122bl Maria Reyes Ventos' apartment in Barcelona; 122bc Richard & Lucille Lewin's house in London designed by Seth Stein; 122r Tristan Auer's apartment in Paris; 123l Sara & Joe Farley's apartment in New York, designed by Asfour Guzy; 123r Antony & Kristen Smithie's kitchen in New York, designed by Amanda Halstead of Halstead Designs Intl; 124al Kristiina Ratia's Connecticut home; 124ar Maria Reyes Ventos' apartment in Barcelona; 124b Mr Burke's kitchen designed by Courtney Sloane and Alternative Design; 124–25 a house in London designed by Nico Rensch; 125 Tristan Auer's apartment in Paris; 126a an apartment in Paris designed by Frédéric Méchiche; 126b Jamie Drake's apartment in New York; 127 Mr Burke's kitchen designed by Courtney Sloane and Alternative Design; 128 Maria Reyes Ventos' apartment in Barcelona; 129 Mr & Mrs Van Hool's kitchen designed by Claire Bataille & Paul Ibens Design; 130l Mr Burke's kitchen designed by Courtney Sloane and Alternative Design; 130ac Sally Mackereth & Julian Vogel's house in London, designed by Wells Mackereth; 130bc Jamie Drake's apartment in New York; 130r Jean–Marc Vynckier's home in Lille; 131 Jean–Marc Vynckier's home in Lille; 132l Mr & Mrs Forrester's kitchen, designed by Johnny Grey; 132r a house in the Hamptons designed by Solis Betancourt; 133l Sara & Joe Farley's apartment in New York, designed by Asfour Guzy; 133r Beatrice de Lafontaine's kitchen in Knokke, designed by John Pawson; 133b Sarah Featherstone's kitchen in London; 134al Antony & Kristen Smithie's kitchen in New York, designed by Amanda Halstead of Halstead Designs Intl; 134cl Maria Reyes Ventos' apartment in Barcelona; 134ar Maxime & Athénais d'Angeac's home in Paris; 134ba house in London designed by Nico Rensch; 135al Jamie Drake's apartment in New York; 135ar Mr & Mrs Van Hool's kitchen designed by Claire Bataille & Paul Ibens Design; 135bl Dominique Kieffer's apartment in Paris; 135br Mr & Mrs Moscowitz' kitchen designed by Vicente Wolf; 136 Sophie Douglas of Fusion Design & Architecture's converted barn in Somerset; 136b Antony & Kristen Smithie's kitchen in New York, designed by Amanda Halstead of Halstead Designs; 137 Harding Residence, with architecture by Audrey Matlock Architects; 138a Maria Reyes Ventos' apartment in Barcelona; 138bl Penny Duncan's kitchen in London; 138–39 Sara & Joe Farley's apartment in New York, designed by Asfour Guzy; 139l Mr & Mrs Forrester's kitchen, designed by Johnny Grey; 139br Todd & Amy Hase's Bridgehampton house; 140a Harding Residence, with architecture by Audrey Matlock Architects; 140c Maria Reyes Ventos' apartment in Barcelona; 140b Sophie Douglas of Fusion Design & Architecture's converted barn in Somerset; 141a Mr & Mrs Van Hool's kitchen designed by Claire Bataille & Paul Ibens Design; 141bl private residence, Soho, New York, Shamir Shah Design; 141br Tristan Auer's apartment in Paris; 142al private residence, Soho, New York, Shamir Shah Design; 142ar & cl Mr & Mrs Forrester's kitchen, designed by Johnny Grey; 142cl a kitchen in Belgium designed by Fahrenheit; 142bl Beatrice de Lafontaine's kitchen in Knokke, designed by John Pawson; 142br Maxime & Athénais d'Angeac's home in Paris; 143l a house in London designed by Gordana Mandic of Buildburo; 143r Evi Kalogianni Bouras' kitchen in London, designed by Adjaye & Associates; 144a private residence, Soho, New York, Shamir Shah Design; 144bl Sarah Featherstone's kitchen in London; 144br a house in London designed by Gordana Mandic of Buildburo; 145a Mr & Mrs Van Hool's kitchen designed by Claire Bataille & Paul Ibens Design;

photographic credits

145bl and br Sara & Joe Farley's apartment in New York, designed by Asfour Guzy; 146a a house in New York designed by Shelton, Mindel & Associates; 146bl Peter Wheeler & Pascale Revert's London home, designed by Eric Gizard; 146br Maria Reyes Ventos' apartment in Barcelona; 147al Mr & Mrs Moscowitz' kitchen designed by Vicente Wolf; 147ac a house in New York designed by Shelton, Mindel & Associates; 147bl Sarah Featherstone's kitchen in London; 147bc Sara & Joe Farley's apartment in New York, designed by Asfour Guzy; 147r Suzanne Tick & Terry Mowers' apartment in New York; 148–50 a house in the Hamptons designed by Solis Betancourt; 152a Marta Ventos' apartment in Barcelona; 153 Keith & Cathy Abell's New York house designed by 1100 Architect; 154a a house in London designed by Lynne Fornieles of Febo Designs; 154br Richard & Lucille Lewin's house in London designed by Seth Stein; 155 Mark and Cynthia Wilkinson's kitchen in Wiltshire; 156–57 main pic Harding Residence, with archi-tecture by Audrey Matlock Architects; 160l Beatrice de Lafontaine's kitchen in Knokke, designed by John Pawson; 160r Sara & Joe Farley's apart-ment in New York, designed by Asfour Guzy; 161r Dominique Kieffer's apartment in Paris; 162al Penny Duncan's kitchen in London; 162ar Angela Carr's house in London, designed by Azman Owens; 162bl a house in the Hamptons designed by Solis Betancourt; 163 Kristiina Ratia's Connecticut home; 164 Angela Carr's house in London, designed by Azman Owens; 165 Kristiina Ratia's Connecticut home; 169l Todd & Amy Hase's Bridgehampton house; 171 Beatrice de Lafontaine's kitchen in Knokke, designed by John Pawson; 172 private res-idence, Soho, New York, Shamir Shah Design; 172 inset Dominique Kieffer's apartment in Paris; 173 Maria Reyes Ventos' apartment in Barcelona; 174 Tony Baratta's house in Long Island; 175a & bl Sally Mackereth & Julian Vogel's house in London, designed by Wells Mackereth; 175r Maria Reyes Ventos' apartment in Barcelona; 176–177 main pic Mr & Mrs Van Hool's kitchen designed by Claire Bataille & Paul Ibens Design; 178a Mr & Mrs Moscowitz' kitchen designed by Vicente Wolf; 178bc Mr Burke's kitchen designed by Courtney Sloane and Alternative Design; 178br Tony Baratta's house in Long Island; 179 Maria Reyes Ventos' apartment in Barcelona; 180a Evi Kalogianni Bouras' kitchen in London, designed by Adjaye & Associates; 181l a house in the Hamptons designed by Solis Betancourt; 182–83 a house in London designed by Nico Rensch; 185 Tony Baratta's house in Long Island; 186 Maxime & Athénais d'Angeac's home in Paris; 189 Mr & Mrs Forrester's kitchen, designed by Johnny Grey.

Companies and individuals whose work is featured in this book:

1100 Architects
435 Hudson Street
New York, NY 10014, USA
001.212.645.1011
www.1100architect.com
pages 13l, 153

Abstrakt Architects
8 rue d'Enghien
75010 Paris
00.33.1.40.22.93.09
pages 36–37

Adjaye & Associates
27 Sunbury Workshops,
Swanfield Street, London W2
020 7739 4969
pages 84–87, 143r, 180a

Alternative Design
Courtney Sloane
21 West Street
Garden Level, New York
NY 10011, USA
001.646.230.7222
www.alternativedesign.com
pages 127, 130l

Alternative Plans
9 Hester Road
Battersea Bridge
London SW11 4AN
020 7228 6460
www.alternative-plans.co.uk
pages 38–41

Architeam
(Nico Rensch)
Campfield House
Powdermill Lane
Battle
East Sussex TN33 0SY
07711 412898
www.architeam.co.uk
pages 13r, 182–183

Asfour Guzy
594 Broadway
Suite 1204
New York
NY 10012, USA
001.212.334.9350
www.asfourguzy.com
pages 74–77, 138–39b, 145 bl

Audrey Matlock
88 West Broadway
New York
NY 10007, USA
001.212.267.2378
www.audreymatlockarchitect.com
pages 137, 156–57

Azman Owens Architects
18 Charlotte Road,
London EC2A 3PB
020 7739 8191
www.azmanowens.com
pages 42–45, 80–83

Buildburo
Gordana Mandic
7 Tecott Road
London SW10 0SA
020 7352 1092
www.buildburo.co.uk
pages 68–69, 143l, 144 br

Claire Bataille & Paul Ibens
Designs NV
Vekestraat 13
Bus 14
2000 Antwerp
Belgium
00.32.3.231.3593
bataille.ibens@planetinternet.be
pages 107ar, 129, 141a,
145a, 176–77

Boffi spa
Via Oberdan
70-20030 Lentate sul Seveso,
Italy
00.39.0362.5341
boffimarket@boffi.it
www.boffi.it
pages 38–41, 101ar

Bulthaup
37 Wigmore Street
London W1U 1PP
020 7495 3663
www.bulthaup.com
pages 100-101 main picture

Deirdre Dyson Contemporary
Carpets Limited
331 Kings Road
London SW3 5ES
020 7795 0122
www.deirdredyson.com

Diamond Baratta Design Inc,
270 Lafayette Street
New York
NY 10012, USA
001.212.966.8892
pages 92–95, 174

Dominique Kieffer
(fabric designer)
Les Editions Dominique Kieffer
8 rue Herold, 75001 Paris
00.33.1.42.21.32.44
www.dkieffer.com
pages 17, 32–33

Drake Design Associates
315 East 62nd Street
5th Floor, New York
NY 10021, USA
001.212.754.3099
www.drakedesignassociates.com
pages 2, 126b

Duncan Interiors
Penny Duncan
duncaninteriors@aol.com
07940 543553
pages 6–7

Eric Gizard Associes
14 rue Crespin du Cast,
75011 Paris
00.33.1.55.28.38.58
information@gizardassocies.com
www.gizardassocies.com
pages 108bl, 146bl

Escenas Barcelona S.L.
Maria Reyes Ventos
13 Pedró de la Creu
08017 Barcelona
Tel: 00.34.93.2803.521
pages 49, 128, 173, 179

Fahrenheit
130b Avenue Louise
1000 Brussels, Belgium
00.32.2.644.2800
fahrenheit@fahrenheit.be
www.fahrenheit.be
pages 88–91

Featherstone Associates
74 Clerkenwell Road
London EC1M 5AQ
020 7490 1212
www.featherstone-associates.co.uk
pages 8–9, 117b

Febo Designs
(Lynne Fornieles)
Foxcombe, South Harting
Petersfield, Hampshire
GU31 5PL
01730 825041
febodesigns@btinternet.com
pages 64–67

François Marcq
8 rue Fernand Neuray
1050 Brussels, Belgium
00.32.2.513.1328
Francoismarcq@skynet.be
pages 88–91

Frédéric Méchiche
14 rue Saint Croix de la
Bretonnerie, 75004 Paris
00.33.1.42.78.78.28
pages 56–59

Fusion Design & Architecture
4 Risborough Street
London SE1 0HE
020 7928 9982
www.fusiondna.co.uk
pages 60–61

Halstead Designs International
9 Warwick Square
London SW1V 2AA
020.7834.2511
halsteaddesign@aol.com
pages 123r

Jean-Marc Vynckier
49 rue Daubenton,
59100 Roubaix
Tel: 00.33.3.20.27.86.59
Tov@nordnet.fr
page 131

John Pawson
Unit B, 70–78 York Way
London N1 9AG
020 7837 2929
www.johnpawson.co.uk
pages 18–21, 133ar

Johnny Grey Ltd
Fyning Copse
Rogate
Nr Petersfield
Hampshire GU31 5DH
01730 821424
www.johnnygrey.co.uk
pages 96–99, 112–23, 189

Kristiina Ratia
001.203.852.0027
Kristiinaratia@aol.com
pages 10–11, 28–31, 163

Mark Wilkinson
Overton House, High Street
Bromham, Nr Chippenham

Wiltshire SN15 2HA
01380 850004
pages 110, 120–21

Maxime d'Angeac Architecte
41 rue Puchet, 75017 Paris
00.33.1.53.11.01.82
dangeac@club-internet.fr
pages 142br, 186

MK Architects (Susanne
Mahdavi & Mehid Khorshidian),
22 Dollis Park, London N3 1HN
020 8349 3202
Mkarchitects@postmaster.co.uk
pages 54–55

Original Interieurs Design Corp
Laurence Pichon-Kriegel
loladesign2002@yahoo.com
pages 26–27

Seth Stein Architects
15 Grand Union Centre

West Row
London W10 5AS
020 8968 8581
www.sethstein.com
pages 50-53

Shamir Shah Designs
150 West 28th Street
Suite 1102, New York
NY 10001, USA
001.212.274.7476
shamirshah@earthlink.net
pages 141bl, 144a, 172 main
picture

Shelton Mindel & Associates
143 West 20th Street
New York
NY 10011, USA
001.212.243.3939
pages 114–15 main picture

Smith Caradoc-Hodgkins
Architects

43 Tanner Street
London SE1 3PL
020 7407 0717
www.sch-architects.com
pages 46–47

Solis Betancourt
1739 Connecticut Avenue NW
Washington DC 20009
USA
001.202.659.8734
www.solisbetancourt.com
pages 22–25, 148–150, 181

Suzanne Tick & Terry Mowers
636 Broadway, Room 1200
New York, NY 10012, USA
001.212.598.0611
pages 147r

Todd Hase
261 Spring Street, New York,
NY10013, USA
001.212.334.3568

www.toddhase.com
pages 79, 139br

Tristan Auer
5a Cour de la Metairie
75020 Paris
00.33.1.43.49.57.20
Tristanauer@wanadoo.fr
pages 4–5, 125

Vicente Wolf
333 West 39th Street
New York, NY 10018
001.212 465 0590
pages 70–73

Wells Mackareth Architects
Unit 14, Archer Street Studios
10–11 Archer Street, London
W1D 7AZ
020 7287 5504
hq@wellsmackareth.com
www.wellsmackareth.com
pages 14–15

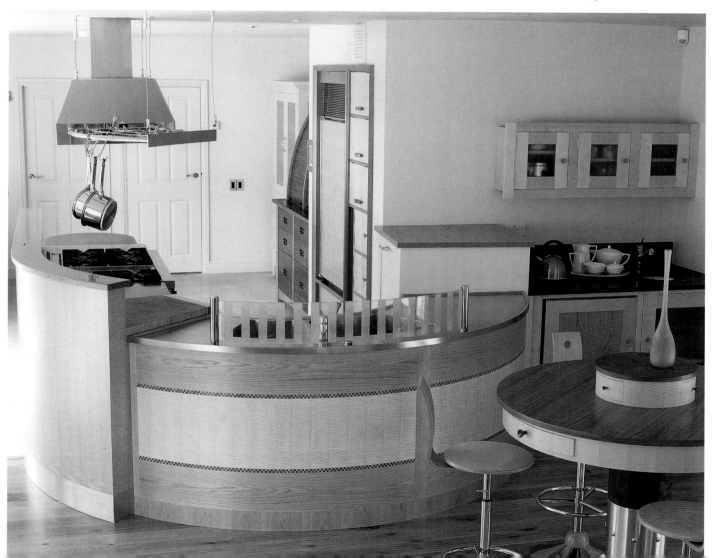

Index

Acknowledgements

Many thanks to all the architects, designers, kitchen planners and PR companies who have been so helpful in putting this book together, and the home owners who allowed photography in their homes. Also, I would like to thank Jacqui Small and Sian Parkhouse, who made working on this book such a pleasure; Andrew Wood for his skills in photography, long-distance driving and map reading; Larraine Shamwana for her design input; and Sandy, who is always there, giving moral support.